Welcome Home

A Journey of Deeper Faith Through Cancer

Carol Cox Taylor

WESTBOW
PRESS®
A DIVISION OF THOMAS NELSON
& ZONDERVAN

Copyright © 2016 Carol Cox Taylor.

All rights reserved. No part of this book may be used or reproduced by any means, graphic, electronic, or mechanical, including photocopying, recording, taping or by any information storage retrieval system without the written permission of the author except in the case of brief quotations embodied in critical articles and reviews.

This book is a work of non-fiction. Unless otherwise noted, the author and the publisher make no explicit guarantees as to the accuracy of the information contained in this book and in some cases, names of people and places have been altered to protect their privacy.

All Scripture quotations in this publications are from The Message. Copyright © by Eugene H. Peterson 1993, 1994, 1995, 1996, 2000, 2001, 2002. Used by permission of NavPress Publishing Group.

Scripture quotations taken from the New American Standard Bible®, Copyright © 1960, 1962, 1963, 1968, 1971, 1972, 1973, 1975, 1977, 1995 by The Lockman Foundation. Used by permission. (www.Lockman.org)

Scripture taken from the New King James Version. Copyright © 1979, 1980, 1982 by Thomas Nelson, Inc. Used by permission. All rights reserved.

WestBow Press books may be ordered through booksellers or by contacting:

WestBow Press
A Division of Thomas Nelson & Zondervan
1663 Liberty Drive
Bloomington, IN 47403
www.westbowpress.com
1 (866) 928-1240

Because of the dynamic nature of the Internet, any web addresses or links contained in this book may have changed since publication and may no longer be valid. The views expressed in this work are solely those of the author and do not necessarily reflect the views of the publisher, and the publisher hereby disclaims any responsibility for them.

Any people depicted in stock imagery provided by Thinkstock are models, and such images are being used for illustrative purposes only. Certain stock imagery © Thinkstock.

ISBN: 978-1-5127-6207-5 (sc)
ISBN: 978-1-5127-6208-2 (hc)
ISBN: 978-1-5127-6206-8 (e)

Library of Congress Control Number: 2016917880

Print information available on the last page.

WestBow Press rev. date: 11/10/2016

I dedicate this book my husband, my children, my grandchildren and to those who need or are seeking hope and a deeper faith in the one who can provide it. My desire is that Jesus Christ be lifted up and that the Father is glorified.

CONTENTS

Acknowledgments ix
Introduction xi

Chapter 1: What I Learned the First Time 1
Chapter 2: Positive Results, Negative News 5
Chapter 3: Unsure of the Next Step 9
Chapter 4: To the Wilderness I Go 14
Chapter 5: That's It 18
Chapter 6: Hitting a Brick Wall 21
Chapter 7: Details Worked Out 25
Chapter 8: Preparation Is the Key 28
Chapter 9: It's Time to Go 32
Chapter 10: Stay Positive 38
Chapter 11: The Waiting Game 43
Chapter 12: A New Body 46
Chapter 13: One Step at a Time 49
Chapter 14: Going Home 52
Chapter 15: Good News, Great God 56
Chapter 16: It's Not Good-bye 59
Chapter 17: Anxiously Counting the Days 64
Chapter 18: Freedom to Laugh Out Loud 68
Chapter 19: Where Love Is 71

Afterword 75

ACKNOWLEDGMENTS

My heart is filled with gratitude toward those who lifted me up to the Father. My faith family at "The Creek" Church kept in constant contact through text messages, Facebook posts, calls, and visits, making sure I never felt alone.

I cannot personally thank all those who came to my aid, because I don't know who they are; many people responded to prayer requests from my friends on Facebook.

My gratitude and respect goes to all the professionals who cared for me from discovery of my illness to post operation. My surgeons and their teams, I feel, are the best in their field.

I would like to thank those who were closest to me on my journey. My husband, Jerry, my children, my in-law children, my grandchildren, and so many other family members were always encouraging me and showing their love. My friend Kim Withrow regularly let me know of her prayers. My Florida friend, Carol Wallace, who talked with me every Tuesday until I was on the other side of this journey.

Last but certainly not least, my friend, Savior, and constant companion, Jesus Christ, who wrapped me in His love and gave me peace like a warm blanket to keep away the shivers of fear. Jesus, all the praise and the glory go to You. You led and carried me. You brought glory to Yourself, and I am humbled that You used me to do that. Your work was a wonder, and I never want to get over it.

INTRODUCTION

There are many kinds of discrimination in our world, but there is one thing that does not discriminate. It does not care who you are, where you live, how much money you have, or about your gender or race.

It is one of the most dreaded words that can be spoken in a doctor's office about yourself or a family member.

I am referring to the C-word, a substitute for what many cannot bear to say: cancer.

Every year the American Cancer Society, the National Cancer Institute, and other organizations report statistics on how many will face this terrible disease, and the increases are staggering. As many as one in three people will deal with this life-altering diagnosis on some level. Apparently it is not a matter of if but when it will happen. How prepared are you, and how prepared can you be?

What happens to your faith if you are a child of God and you hear this word applied to you? Do you lose your faith, or does it become stronger?

At times you must feel your way through the journey of having cancer. I know because I took this journey not once but twice. The second time brought me to a deeper place in my faith. Thank you for looking on as I revisit my memories. I praise the one who was with me every second of the journey. My Savior, Jesus Christ, deserves all the glory for the outcome of this time in my life. Everyone is invited to share in the love of Christ.

CHAPTER 1
What I Learned the First Time

There I was, sitting in the room where I had sat annually for six years. The first time was not so great, and I would soon learn that this visit would not be either. I was reflecting on the first year. I had not expected the outcome of that day.

Women, if you have been through this, you know how it goes. You get your annual mammogram, and a medical professional tells you, "Don't get dressed yet so we can check the pictures." That first trip brought me to a lumpectomy with crystal-clear margins in 2006.

When you get a diagnosis of any disease, you google, you study, and you research what makes it tick. You hope the research helps you understand what you can do or not do to make the disease go away and not return. That is exactly what I did. I am a Google girl, and I put in countless hours online. I studied what cancer is and what it does to the body. I received an education that I would not have chosen, but later I realized that it was a great gift.

I found out about treatments, the side effects of each, and what they do to the body. I learned more about nutrition. I did well for six years. I never looked or felt better.

God led me to many people who helped me and whom I could help with my testimony about what I had experienced. God allowed me to meet and talk to a man named Bill Howell, who believed in holistic healing.

Two years before my cancer, I had started dabbling with the study of herbs versus synthetic medicines, but that was as far as it went until my cancer.

I was amazed at what Bill had learned sixteen years before our meeting. His wife had died of complications from cancer treatments within six months of her diagnosis.

When Bill found himself facing cancer, he decided to do things differently. With the knowledge he gained and with a change in eating habits, among other things, he could say he was cancer-free without the standard treatments. He told me that he had decided he would kill himself or cure himself. God allowed him to learn things that brought him a long, healthy life. He told me that at seventy-three he was stronger and healthier and had more energy than he had had since he was a very young man.

I thank God for bringing Bill into my life when He did. I benefited from this man's years of study and research. I picked his brain at every opportunity.

The first time I talked to Bill we spent forty-five minutes on the phone, and I could have listened to him for the rest of that evening. He spoke of how important it was to keep a balanced pH level. He wholeheartedly believed in supplements of vitamins, nutrients, and minerals in our diets.

It is well known that the American diet is lacking in the elements needed to make our systems healthy. This man drove home the fact that sugar is killing us.

God created our bodies to ward off certain illnesses, but because we bog them down with many things, such as sugar, mucus from excess dairy products, inflammation from irritation, and parasitic activity, our immune systems cannot work properly.

I knew I was a sugar addict and had been since I was a child. I knew I had to change the way I looked at my diet. At first, it was hard. I was afraid to put anything in my mouth that I had not analyzed. Would it hurt me or help to keep me healthy?

I underwent a major life and mind-set change regarding the way I thought about food. I had to make good choices on a daily basis to be healthier.

Not only do we eat food that is bad for us, but we are exposed every day to chemicals in pesticides, cleaning products, smoke, beauty products, and many more items. I know we cannot escape all of this, but I am a firm believer that if we do all that we possibly can, God will do the rest.

I eliminated everything that I felt could make a difference. After researching the effects of aluminum on the brain and the rest of the body, I stopped using deodorant with aluminum. It goes under the arm and straight into the chest where your breasts happen to be. I replaced all of my aluminum cookware with stainless steel or iron. What is soda pop? A chemical sugar liquid in an aluminum can. The only good thing about it is the taste. I know it's a bummer to give up soda, but it is the right choice.

I ate organic meat, vegetables, bread, and dairy products as often as possible. Many people told me, "Oh, I could never do that." I used to think that too.

Doing this was hard, but cancer provides a strong motivation to change the way you think and to take action to improve your health.

You know what they say. "Make it five years, and if your cancer isn't back, you've got it pretty much beat." I did quite well and got to that five-year mark and beyond.

I started to relax a little on my regimen and slipped a bit here and there on my diet. Why are humans like this? Why do we know what to do but don't do it?

Prevention is so much better than trying to fix a problem with your health. A great amount of information is available and easy to find on the Internet. You have to check, cross-reference, and read between the lines in some cases, but it can be done.

No one will take better care of you than you, so become an expert on what you need to learn. I did research for nine years and put together information that I refer back to on a regular basis. This information has kept me balanced and has reminded me what I need to do to be healthier. I have shared it with countless people I have met shopping, communicated with on Facebook, or conversed with when the subject has turned to health. I am passionate about being the best me possible and helping in any way I can to do the same for others.

CHAPTER 2

Positive Results, Negative News

Fast-forward to Tuesday, September 18, 2012, and I sat waiting to have my annual mammogram. My name was called and I was taken to an X-ray room with that big machine every woman who has gotten a mammogram hates to see.

I had learned to count the pictures taken. My right side was my trouble spot, and I noticed the technician took an extra one for that side. I was told to go out, find a seat, and "Don't get dressed until we tell you to." I returned to my seat and watched women coming in and out. All of them were told to get dressed because they were good to go.

A technician showed up at the door and asked me to follow her. They wanted more pictures of my right side.

Afterward, I was told to return to the waiting room but not to get dressed. A few minutes later, the same technician leaned back into the room and again asked me to follow her. She said they wanted me to have an ultrasound. It was like déjà vu. As I walked to the examining room, I knew they had found something.

There were two technicians in the room, and a radiologist entered and did the ultrasound. He told me they had found two small places that looked very suspicious.

I stopped him and asked if my husband could join us from the outer waiting room. Jerry had come with me since the doctor's office was an hour away. I was so thankful he was there. Because he had retired earlier that month, he was able to be home with me.

When Jerry sat down beside me, the doctor told us that he felt a biopsy was crucial.

There was an opening in the schedule for that day at 2:00 p.m. We told him we would take the appointment. It was twelve-forty-five, so we decided to have lunch. After we called all the kids, we went to find a place to eat. At this point I wasn't very hungry, but I knew it would be the best thing to do. It would make the next hour as normal as possible while we waited.

We returned to the clinic, and I was prepared for the procedure. As I lay on my side and the doctor and the nurses went to work, I prayed and wondered what the next few days would bring. During the ultrasound biopsy, markers were put into place just in case I had to have surgery. Then I quickly got dressed, and Jerry and I went straight home.

I returned to a strict regimen of detoxing and cleansing my body. I bought a juicer and began juicing fruits and vegetables. Having studied the benefits of juicing at the end of the previous year, I decided that this was the time to start.

I learned what vitamins were in each vegetable and piece of fruit I juiced. I had found juicing to be healthy and knew I should make it a part of my daily regimen. I was determined to stick with it, keeping in mind that the benefits outweighed the inconvenience. The cleanup was not so bad once I got used to it, and the difference juicing made was amazing.

The radiologist had put a rush on the pathology report. It was not a diagnosis I wanted to hear. For the second time in my life I was told I had cancer, and it had to come out. The radiologist believed the second spot was the same type since it was in about the same area. The doctor's office made an appointment for me with a surgeon for two days later.

Jerry and I returned to the clinic building because the surgeon's office was also located there. The surgeon was a firm believer in chemotherapy, radiation, and hormone treatments. I told him my belief about each and he strongly disagreed. I said that I appreciated his knowledge but that my thoughts were definite on the subject. He also wanted me to have a mastectomy, and I gave him a firm no.

Despite my decision, I would never tell others not to have these treatments. If you feel that you need them and that this is the path of healing for you, go ahead with it. Listen to God and do exactly what He tells you to do.

Scripture shows that God healed the blind in different ways. In some cases He made mud mixed with His saliva and applied it to their eyes. Some He touched, and some He healed with the power of His word.

Make sure it is your decision and not some medical opinion being pushed on you. More than likely, your cancer has been there for quite a while, and a few days spent researching what is best for you won't make a difference. It may be hard to concentrate, but you need to explore all options and make an educated choice.

I told the surgeon I wanted another lumpectomy with no follow-up treatment. He told me I was foolish, and I said he had a right to his opinion. I did go through with the surgery, and it was of great benefit to me, but that may be the subject for another book.

Two days after the surgery, a breast cancer counselor called me. We had met six years earlier and had become good friends. She told me that my borders were not clear and that I needed more surgery to be free of the cancer that remained in my body. I was very disappointed, but I was still going to trust in what the Lord was doing in my life. I believe that everything happens for a reason and that all things are turned to the good for the child of God, no matter what.

I decided to make the hour's drive to the clinic to get all of my records.

I knew deep in my heart that I shouldn't have my surgery in

the same town. I felt that I needed to find a new place to continue my care and to undergo a second surgery, but I didn't know where.

I prayed and asked God to show me where to go or to send me someone who could give me direction. No sooner did I ask than my daughter-in-law, Kandis, told me of a place about an hour and a half away. Her stepmother went there when she found a lump, and she loved the medical staff. I got the name and the phone number of a doctor.

I called the same day I received the information and got an appointment about two weeks from that date. I was very excited about making the contact and felt I was well on my way to a recovery. Little did I know how long a road it would be.

CHAPTER 3

Unsure of the Next Step

On Tuesday, October 16, Jerry and I made the hour-and-a-half drive to meet another doctor. He was kind and understanding. He wanted me to go through extensive testing, and I agreed to his plan.

I knew that this was the right direction and that I would walk by faith each step of the way.

On Friday, October 19, I returned for a bone scan, a CT scan, and an MRI, which revealed a tiny white spot in my trouble area.

I had always read Scripture, but a time like this made me dig a little deeper. I found many passages that spoke to me, and I leaned on them heavily during this period. The quiet times felt less rushed and much sweeter. I gained a clearer understanding of what was most important, and the other things seemed to fall away.

In a Facebook message, Tara, my oldest daughter, sent me a devotion written by Charles Spurgeon that she had found. I received it on a day when I felt I needed a word from the Lord. It is such a blessing when we need a word and get it in perfect timing. This is God's timing, not ours. In part the devotion read,

> Psalm 81:10 KJV: "Open thy mouth wide, and I will fill it."
>
> What an encouragement to pray! Our human notions would lead us to ask small things because our deservings are so small, but the Lord would have us request great blessings. Prayer should be as simple

a matter as the opening of the mouth; it should be a natural, unconstrained utterance. When a man is earnest he opens his mouth wide, and our text urges us to be fervent in our supplications.

Yet it also means that we may make bold with God and ask many and large blessings at His hands. Because the Lord has given us so much, He invites us to ask for more, yea, to expect more.

See how the little birds in their nests seems to be all mouth when the mother comes to feed them. Let it be the same with us. Let us take in grace at every door. Let us drink it in as a sponge sucks up the water in which it lies. God is ready to fill us if we are only ready to be filled. Let our needs make us open our mouths; let our faintness cause us to open our mouths and pant, yea, let our alarm make us open our mouths with a child's cry. The opened mouth shall be filled by the Lord Himself. So be it unto us, O Lord, this day.

I found another devotion that spoke volumes to me. I had been doing a lot of reading and digging. Isn't that how it happens? We are going along, and wham, we hit a spiritual speed bump or pothole that causes us to slow down or even to stop to change a spiritual flat tire.

Here are some of the Scripture verses I found that helped to encourage me.

"But those who suffer He delivers in their suffering; He speaks to them in their affliction. He is wooing you from the jaws of distress to a spacious place, free from restriction, to the comfort of your table laden with choice food" (Job 30:15–16 NIV).

"He brought me into a spacious place; He rescued me because He delighted in me" (Psalm 18:19 NIV).

"You have not handed me over to the enemy but have set my feet in a spacious place" (Psalm 31:8 NIV).

After reading all these passages with the common denominator of a spacious place, I wanted to dig a little more. I learned that the Hebrew word *ravach* means "to breathe freely, to revive, to have ample room, to be refreshed." What wonderful treasure God has hidden in His Word that we can find with a little digging.

I didn't know that I needed a spacious place, but God promised it to me long before the day of my first mammogram. When the walls seem to be closing in, a spacious place is a wonderful thing to have. I praise the Lord for the spacious place He gave me.

On October 22, I received a call from my doctor's nurse. They had the results of the bone and CT scans. They couldn't find any cancer in my body, and I was elated. The nurse told me they wanted to do a needle biopsy on the spot that had showed up on the MRI. Surgery was still on the table to get me clear borders on all sides and to drain some fluid buildup, but overall this was good news.

I had amazing family and friends who were there for me. They called, sent messages, prayed, and showed great support from start to finish. My pastors and pastor friends called and came by the hospital and to our home to encourage me with Scripture and prayer.

It is so important not to go through something like this alone. I had one friend, Carol, who committed to be there for me day or night whenever I needed her. She promised to call me every Tuesday to check up on me.

I was so blessed to have loved ones to share my thoughts and feelings with. I wrote in blog form on my Facebook wall. The practice was therapeutic. It allowed friends to stay up to date and kept me focused as I recorded events.

On October 24, I returned for my needle biopsy. I was nervous. In the last few months I had been in tight enclosed places for CT scans and MRIs. Knowing I was about to be in another such place, face down and having to stay completely still for fifty-five minutes during my MRI needle biopsy, I asked the Lord to remind about a spacious place He had given me.

I looked up when the technician left the room just before putting a port in my arm, and did a double take. There, hanging on the wall to my left, was a print showing a woman walking in an open field filled with flowers.

I would like to think God intended that I should see that print when someone purchased it for the clinic.

As I lay face down and immobile for nearly an hour during the biopsy, that picture and a song by Luther Bridgers kept coming to mind.

> "Feasting on the riches of His grace,
> Resting 'neath His sheltering wing,
> Always looking on His smiling face,
> That is why I shout and sing.
> Jesus, Jesus, Jesus,
> Sweetest name I know,
> Fills my every longing,
> Keeps me singing as I go.
> Though sometimes He leads through waters deep,
> Trials fall across the way;
> Though sometimes the path seems rough and steep,
> See His footprints all the way."

My nervousness was gone, replaced with peace. I was not in there alone. Jesus was with me, as He was with the three Hebrew children in Deuteronomy. He will be with you too. Just ask.

The nurses and the technician said they had never seen someone remain so still that long. One of them said, "People just have to move when they are told not to." They asked me how I did it. I simply said I was praying and praising the Lord for His goodness.

My whole desire while going through this procedure, and throughout the journey God allowed me to take, was that He would show His strength and would get the glory for whatever took place. By nature, I am not a vocal person, but I have definitely become one. I became a brave person during my journey through cancer, not because I stood alone but because of who stood with me. I was like a small child who is being bullied on the playground and sees his big brother approaching. Suddenly the child discovers a bravery that was not there in the absence of his brother and feels he can take on the world because he can draw on newfound strength.

My big brother, Jesus, was with me every step of the way. Was that not His promise? Deuteronomy 31:6 says, "Be strong and courageous. Do not be afraid or terrified because of them, for the Lord your God goes with you; he will never leave you nor forsake you." I leaned on that promise and many more throughout my illness. I didn't have a blueprint, a map, or a plan of action other than trusting the One I knew would not leave me. I didn't know my future, but I knew the one who did. I found peace in the middle of a whirlwind of uncertainty.

CHAPTER 4

To the Wilderness I Go

When you have cancer or face any other threat to your life, you experience a new clarity. You become aware of what really matters. My prayer is that I will never lose this clarity. I have the battle scars to remind me, but then again, I am human.

We go through the same cycle the Israelites did when they were in the wilderness. God blesses us; we praise, soon forget, get into trouble, and call out to God. He delivers us and the process starts all over again. My heart's desire is that I never get over what He did for me and through me.

They put a rush on the needle biopsy and scheduled an appointment with my doctor the next day at 3:00 p.m. I was anxious to hear what he had to say. I was still on a high from the results of my bone scan and other testing. I was ready for this ordeal to be over.

Jerry and I arrived and were shown to a consultation room with a big white board. Little did I know that board would change my life even more.

I sat down in one of the chairs, and Jerry sat to my left. The doctor entered the room and we said our hellos. He said that he had a lot of information for us and that we could ask questions anytime we wanted.

He started by discussing the little white spot they had found. It was cancer, small but cancer. I thought, *I still have cancer in my body, and that means more surgery for sure.* No sooner did I think it than the doctor said I would have to have more surgery.

He turned and started to draw on the board. On the far left of the board, he sketched a woman's upper torso and in drawing cut away some of the right breast. The doctor did an outline of my second lumpectomy, which I'd had just the month before, drew a big X over it, and said, "This can no longer be you."

He then told me I needed a mastectomy. There it was, the word I had dreaded. I was stunned and devastated. The doctor made another drawing showing what a mastectomy looked like. He explained what would happen during the procedure and how he planned to do it. With a third drawing on the far right of the board, he depicted treatments and reconstruction methods that he would present.

I tried to grasp what the doctor was saying as he bombarded us with all this information. All I could think about was how I could buy a bra that fit, what I would look like in a bathing suit, and what my husband would think when he looked at me.

As the doctor spoke, all I wanted to do was cry. I had a knot in my throat that hurt. It would not leave, and I thought I was choking. I wanted to run away.

I then thought of Jerry. I had studied all these words and terms for several years now. I could not imagine what my husband was thinking. All I knew was that this would be a long, messy process, and I wasn't sure what getting to the other side would involve or what I would look like once I was there.

I told the doctor that he had given me a lot to think about and that I wanted the rest of the week and the weekend to consider everything and to pray. He agreed but encouraged me to make my decision so surgery could be scheduled. He said I could call his nurse about my decision on surgery and reconstruction plans. I did not know where to begin to think about it all.

We left the clinic and I started crying as soon as we entered the car. I could not stop. My poor husband took me to Red

Lobster to try to cheer me up. We had planned to eat there the next time we were in the area.

This restaurant was always a treat since we did not have one in our town. I knew what Jerry was doing and I loved him for it. I was not hungry at all, but I went along with him because he had made the effort.

By this time all the kids had been notified, and each wanted to talk with me while we were in the restaurant. Every time I spoke to one of them, I started to cry. They all gave me their best "It's going to be okay," and I knew that deep down, but the news about what lay ahead was still raw for me.

I am a Christian, but I am a human being too, so I allowed myself this little breakdown. Our poor waiter probably didn't know what to think. I could just imagine him thinking my husband and I were having a huge fight.

Weeks earlier, I had discovered a song called "Home" by Phillip Phillips. He was the newest *American Idol* winner, and that was his winning song. I adopted it as my theme song. It was upbeat and had an awesome message.

I went to our local Walmart, purchased his CD, and played that song over and over. One of the things I did for exercise was to march to that song in my house. Yes, march. Around my big kitchen, down the hall, through the living room I would go. I would turn up the music to hear the words.

> "Settle down; it'll all be clear.
> Don't pay no mind to the demons; they fill you with fear.
> The trouble it might drag you down.
> If you get lost, you can always be found.
> Just know you're not alone,
> 'Cause I'm gonna make this place your home."

I felt the Lord speaking to me in that song. The grandkids got on board with it too. They would turn it on and march with me. What a spectacle we would make! To this day when I hear "Home," I feel it is my battle cry.

I had a big decision to make. The doctor's words had shocked me, but I had to get back on track. I had my emotional moments if I let my mind wonder, so I tried to stay focused. I never wavered in my trust in the Lord. I still had peace deep down in my soul, remembering Job's words: "Though He slay me, yet will I trust Him."

The situation had not turned out how I wanted or prayed for, but I still believed that "all things work together for the good" for those who love God.

Worry not only shows that we don't trust God, but it robs us of the victory we can gain by letting God be real in our lives. We must live like we believe that God is our help. I didn't want to give up a part of me that I had had for fifty-two years, but I knew the Lord would be faithful.

I had to decide about extensive surgery, and the reconstruction options did not sit well with me at all. I wanted to have surgery and to be done with it. I did not look forward to months of stretching followed by implants. I did not like the idea of having something foreign in my body. It was a bit overwhelming. I prayed for clarity of mind in deciding what I should do. It wasn't long before something was brought to my remembrance.

All I had to go on was one statement the doctor had made in his presentation in the consultation room. He had said something about using my own body tissue. What did that look like? What did that encompass? Being the Google girl that I am, I typed in "reconstruction using your own body tissue." I had no idea what I was looking for, but I felt like I was on the right track in finding it.

CHAPTER 5
That's It

With that search, I found two types of surgeries. The more I read, the more excited I got. I had found it! This was the surgery that I needed. I learned that one surgery used stomach muscle, a TRAM flap, and another, the DIEP flap procedure, did not.

Since I had six grandkids and didn't want to risk a hernia every time I picked one of them up, I knew the DIEP flap was for me. DIEP stands for "deep inferior epigastric perforators," and the procedure involves microsurgery.

My reading made it clear that having this surgery and finding someone who could perform it would be a long shot that depended on the clinic and my doctor. I found the information on Friday after the clinic closed, so I had to wait until Monday morning to call. I could hardly wait.

I knew this was the answer, and I thanked the Lord for leading me on the right path. God is in the details. We must do all we can, and God will always do the rest. We just have to be willing to follow. During this time I often sang a little song I had learned as a child.

"The Lord knows the way through the wilderness. All I have to do is follow."

This is so true. We have to trust that He loves us and always wants the best for us.

I did more research on surgeons who performed this type of surgery. I learned that it would take eight to ten hours, but that didn't matter to me. This meant I might have my mastectomy and reconstruction in one day. I was elated.

I also learned that everything used in reconstruction would come from me, and I would get a mini tummy tuck to boot. I had had three children, including twins, and my stomach was not pretty with all of the stretch marks. I liked the idea of the tummy tuck and thought of it as a perk of this kind of surgery.

Monday came and I called as soon as I thought the clinic had opened. I reached the doctor's nurse with the number I had been given. I told her who I was and said I had decided to have the mastectomy. Then I asked her if there was a surgeon who could do the DIEP flap. She said no but that the surgeons in this practice did the TRAM flap. I told her I had researched that surgery but wanted the DIEP. She told me she was sorry but that couldn't be done through the clinic.

I asked the nurse if she knew anyone who did the DIEP flap or where I could find someone, and she immediately said Vanderbilt University Medical Center. I asked if she had a number for the plastic surgery department and she did. I took down the number and thanked her for her help.

I immediately dialed and reached a receptionist. She was kind and understanding. She transferred me to a plastic surgeon's office. When I hung up the phone, I had an appointment.

I was happy with the way things were working out. In three weeks and one day, I would find out if I was a good candidate for the surgery God had led me to seek. In my heart, I already knew the answer.

Three weeks and one day later, Jerry and I were in the car headed three hours south. Little did we know how often we would make this trip back and forth. We would spend a lot of time in that car. I didn't like the reason, but I loved traveling with my husband. Sometimes we would spend the night because of early appointments.

Surgery of this nature takes great preparation. I would soon learn that I had to have preliminary testing. The first surgery would be about two hours, and the second could take as much as eight.

I would have to remain in the hospital for five nights to be closely monitored for infection and for rejection of tissue. I would come home with three drains. I dreaded this prospect, but I had to go through the ordeal to get through it. I needed to ready my mind for what was coming. I could study up on some things, but I knew I had no clue about others. I would have to walk by faith on those things, knowing that the Lord had a plan.

I met with my plastic surgeon that day. He was understanding of my situation. After asking me some questions and examining me, he said I would be an excellent candidate for the DIEP flap. He fully explained the process and asked me if I had a surgeon to do the first part, which included the mastectomy.

My heart sank when I told him I did not. He left the examining room to check if a colleague was available. She had left for the day, so he made an appointment for me to return to see her. It was scheduled for one week later on November 27. I was one step closer to my surgery, and I felt good about that.

As we drove home, my mind was in overdrive concerning what would happen on the next trip to Nashville. I wondered how many trips we would make before the big day. I resolved to find out all I could about what to expect in the coming weeks.

CHAPTER 6
Hitting a Brick Wall

To keep the appointment with my potential surgeon, we knew we would have to spend the night in Nashville. We would have to get up very early at home to make the 8:00 a.m. appointment. I was a little nervous about meeting yet another new doctor. This was another hurdle to surmount before everything was in place.

Still, I was excited to meet the surgeon. She was accomplished and at the top of her field. I counted it a blessing to have this knowledge of her before meeting her. We arrived at 7:45 a.m., fifteen minutes early. Mine was the first appointment of the day.

After check-in, we took our seats in the waiting room. We were called in at 8:05 a.m. Jerry and I waited for the doctor and her assistant to enter the examining room.

When they came in and the introductions took place, and I felt uneasy. The doctor was pleasant, but I sensed a sort of distance that I couldn't quite understand. I chalked it up to our first-time meeting and to a personality difference.

We discussed my cancer and she quickly asked me, "Why did you not do follow-ups and treatments as suggested?" I was surprised and taken aback. She told me that if I did not plan to go through with the suggested treatments, she could not be a part of this surgery.

My heart sank. The doctor said she was sorry that it seemed I had "hit a wall." I knew something was wrong and there was miscommunication somewhere. I told her my feeling about treatments, but I assured her I had done follow-ups, tests, and lab checks for the previous six years—every four months for the first two years, every six months for the next two, and then annually.

She was confused and asked her assistant why she did not have all of the reports. The doctor didn't think this would affect her decision and stressed again the importance of continuing treatments.

I told her of my feelings on the subject and said I believed I was making the best decision for me.

The doctor excused herself and left the room. Her assistant remained, and I quickly asked, "Do you think she was serious about not doing my surgery?" She said yes.

I looked at Jerry, and he gave me assurance that everything was okay. Deep down I knew that it was, but I didn't see it at the time. Jerry said, "We will find someone else."

I asked the assistant if someone else at Vanderbilt would be willing to do the surgery. She replied with a maybe.

The surgeon returned and apologized for the interruption. It was clear she had also been thrown off balance. She took a seat across from me and asked if I would consider treatment. I told her I would pray about it but would not promise anything at the moment.

I told her that I knew I was where I needed to be, that I had peace when I walked through the door, and that I knew she was my surgeon. She asked if I would be willing to talk to an oncologist, and I said I would talk to anyone she wanted me to see.

She excused herself, and this time the assistant went with her. After a few minutes, the assistant came back and asked if we could return to the waiting room until they set up the meeting with the oncologist.

Jerry and I went to the waiting room. I told him to call our oldest daughter to pray and left for the ladies room. I sent a text to my sister-in-law, Linda, who is my standby prayer warrior, simply saying, "Pray now. God knows."

I hit my knees on the bathroom floor and said a simple prayer. It went something like this. "Lord, You have brought me on this journey. All that I have asked is that You get the glory from my life and that You show Your strength, especially to those who don't know You or who are distant from You. I need an answer from You now about this situation. Please change minds and hearts now. In the name of Jesus."

As soon as I left the ladies room I saw Jerry motioning for me with his arm. They had called my name to see the oncologist. Jerry remained in the waiting room, and I walked with the nurse down the hall.

I was shown to a room and remained there for about two minutes before the oncologist entered. She was a pretty lady with a bright smile. She introduced herself and sat in the chair across from me.

The conversation was pleasant enough. The doctor asked me about myself and wanted to know what had brought me to this facility. She then asked why I did not want to do follow-up treatments after my previous cancer.

I told her of my research and said I had made my decision based on what I had felt and had learned. She asked why I did not undergo hormone treatment after my first cancer. She wondered if I knew that the cancer might not have returned if I had had this treatment. I told her *might* was the key word.

I said six years had passed and I had remained in great health. I told her that my bones, my heart, my veins, my kidneys, my lungs, and my liver were all healthy and that I did not have to take drugs to deal with the side effects of treatments.

I told her I was fifty-two years old and felt great. "I just have cancer," I added, and we both laughed because of the way I said this. I said that I had the utmost respect for her knowledge in her area of study and that I appreciated what she was trying to do. I also told her that I had heard the same advice before but that I had to do what I felt the Lord wanted me to do.

She asked me if I would at least consider hormone treatment. I told her I would pray about it but would make no promises. She gave me a big smile and excused herself.

After about five minutes she returned and told me to follow her. She took me to another waiting room, told me to have a seat, and said someone would take me to pre-op in a few minutes. She wished me well, and I gave her a good-bye hug.

As I waited, my mind went in different directions. I reasoned with myself, saying, *She did say pre-op. What does that mean? What's next? Who am I going to see?* I prayed and thanked the Lord for the peace I felt.

When the nurse came for me, I asked if someone could get my husband, and she said, "Yes, of course." She left me in a small room and went to find Jerry. She quickly returned with him and showed him into the room. He took the chair next to mine and asked, "What is going on?" I told him that I wasn't sure but that this was pre-op. Speaking the words made my heart jump.

A nurse arrived and had me read and sign papers. She told me what to expect, making a copy of each paper and handing it to me. One paper had a line with the words "Surgeon's signature." I looked closely because it was signed. My surgeon's name was on the line!

I wanted to jump out of my seat but tried to remain calm as possible. God had done it. Her mind was changed! She would do the surgery. One of the biggest hurdles was now crossed, and I praised the Lord.

CHAPTER 7
Details Worked Out

I was told I would be notified about when my surgery would be. The schedulers had to coordinate with all the doctors and take their appointments into account to make everything work. I left walking on air. God did something big that day, and I praise Him every time I think of it.

I am reminded of the fall of Jericho. Here's how Scripture tells the story.

> Jericho was shut up tight as a drum because of the People of Israel: no one going in, no one coming out. God spoke to Joshua, "Look sharp now. I've already given Jericho to you, along with its king and its crack troops. Here's what you are to do: March around the city, all your soldiers. Circle the city once. Repeat this for six days. Have seven priests carry seven ram's horn trumpets in front of the Chest.
>
> On the seventh day march around the city seven times, the priests blowing away on the trumpets. And then, a long blast on the ram's horn—when you hear that, all the people are to shout at the top of their lungs. The city wall will collapse at once. All the people are to enter, every man straight on in" ...
>
> Joshua had given orders to the people, "Don't shout. In fact, don't even speak—not so much as a whisper until you hear me say, 'Shout!'-then shout away!" ... When the seventh day came, they got up early and marched around the city this same way but seven times—yes, this day they circled the city seven times. On the seventh time

around the priests blew the trumpets and Joshua signaled the people, "Shout!—God has given you the city!" ...

When the people heard the blast of the trumpets, they gave a thunderclap shout. The wall fell at once. The people rushed straight into the city and took it. (Joshua 6:1–5, 10, 15–16, 20 MSG)

When the Evil One puts up walls, we must be silent. God will deliver us and allow us a shout of victory. The King has given us marching orders, and we must follow them to the letter.

God brought down a wall for me; the surgeon herself had called it a wall. It fell in a matter of minutes. I praise the Lord for toppling that wall. Your wall may take a little longer to come down, but do not get discouraged. God knows your situation, and He loves you. With His help you can face anything.

We were proceeding as planned, and God deserved the glory for that.

I would have to return three days later, which meant another three-hour trip, but that was fine by me. I needed to undergo preliminary testing for the kind of surgery I was to have.

Those tests included blood-work labs, a chest X-ray, and an EKG. I then was scheduled for one more visit three days later. This time I would meet with both surgeons and would have a CT scan to map out my veins. My plastic surgeon didn't want any surprises in the middle of the operation.

I came home knowing that everything was in place for my surgery, but I learned that the mastectomy and the reconstruction could not be done on the same day. The reconstruction was too complex, and my plastic surgeon said he wanted his team to be fresh because of the length of the surgery. The mastectomy would take around two hours and the reconstruction about eight hours.

I was a little disappointed, but I understood. My plan had been to go to sleep with a breast and to wake up with one. That was not going to happen, but it was okay. I headed home to await dates for my surgeries. That was all I needed now. I was happy that God had sent me this way and that everything was falling into place.

I had lost a job earlier in the year due to a budget cut, and Jerry was home for good after retiring, so we had much more time to be together. Little did we know at the time of his retirement that he would be chauffeuring me from one town to another for the next five months. But God works out the details in advance and we have to have faith and believe that.

CHAPTER 8

Preparation Is the Key

I tried to prepare myself for surgery as much as possible. I read the Scriptures, and my quiet times were that much sweeter. I exercised, ate as healthily as I could, and built up my immune system with juicing, staying away from sugars. I continued to march to my theme song, "Home."

> "Settle down; it'll all be clear.
> Don't pay no mind to the demons; they fill you with fear.
> The trouble it might drag you down.
> If you get lost, you can always be found.
> Just know you're not alone,
> 'Cause I'm gonna make this place your home."

Since I was not working, I got to spend more time with my mother. After suffering a stroke almost six years before, she was totally paralyzed on her left side and could not turn over in bed by herself. She was almost completely blind from glaucoma. We kept her home the first year, but she lost all her strength and it was increasingly hard to care for her. Until my layoff, I worked in the town where the nursing home was located, and it was wonderful to be able to visit Mom every day after work.

I would pamper her, washing her face, brushing her hair, or reading Scripture to her. She loved her Bible. I would feed her when her evening meal arrived, but by this time she was eating less. Her health had begun to decline.

We would have wonderful conversations or would enjoy old

movies on her TV. She seemed to speak less each day. She once asked me if I would get mad if she flew away. A knot formed in my throat, but with the clearest voice I could muster, I told her to fly if she wanted to and I would not get mad. She was tired and wanted to go home to heaven.

I did not know how to tell her about my surgery. She was more like a child at this point, and I hated to leave her for any length of time. I was torn between telling her so she could prepare for my absence and saying nothing and having the attendants tell her I would be back soon.

My beautiful, elegant, graceful mother was a shell of herself. This grieved me sometimes. Weeks before my surgery, there were times when I wanted to share the news with her so she could tell me everything would be fine, but I couldn't bring myself to do it. She was the child now, and I had to reassure her. Our roles were reversed, and I was looking out for her and protecting her from fearful things.

One evening the dietitian asked if I could attend a meeting concerning Mom's health. She said the meeting could be scheduled for that day if I could remain at the care center while she arranged for others to attend. I told her I could stay, and I waited about thirty minutes.

I joined the center administrator, the dietitian, the head nurse, and two others for the meeting. They were concerned about Mom's weight loss from lack of eating and encouraged me and my family to let them install a feeding tube. I balked at first. I did not want my mother to lose her ability to eat. It was the only pleasure she had left.

She loved the soft peanut butter fudge I would make her and the strawberry milkshakes I would bring from the local Dairy Queen. The group assured me that if Mom wanted to eat something she could still do that. This procedure would allow the staff to supplement what she ate. I said I would talk with my brother and sister to ask what they thought.

I found it increasingly hard to leave Mom each day, and I did so with a heavy heart. I would get in my car and make the thirty-five-minute drive home. I would pray, sing, and sometimes cry, but I always knew God had everything worked out.

Each day I would listen for my phone to ring or check on the hospital website for my surgery dates. Finally, one day I logged on and the dates January 16 and January 17 were staring back at me. I was happy at last to know when my surgeries would take place.

I shouted for Jerry and called all the kids. The surgeries were still almost a month away, but they were scheduled. They would come after Christmas and New Year's, so I had some breathing room. I had put up my Christmas tree early in November because I didn't know the dates, but I did now! I started to plan my post-surgery wardrobe.

I knew I would have at least three drains, maybe four. I scoured all the websites for information about DIEP flaps and read the chat-room conversations of those who had undergone the procedure.

I got tips on what to do and what not to do. Jerry cut a few extra-large T-shirts down the front for me to wear as cover-ups; they were like short housecoats. I read that yoga pants were ideal to wear because they were made of stretchy material. I knew I didn't need anything binding. My wardrobe would consist of loose clothing, though I didn't know for how long.

Jerry bought me a Velcro belt, and we created a makeshift pocket holder for my drains. I didn't see how those surgical camisoles would work, at least not for me. I prepared as much as possible. I was a girl scout as a child, and that experience is still very much a part of me.

I talked with my brother and sister, and we decided that Mom should have the feeding tube. There were several dry runs, and delays occurred because of scheduling, because Mom's blood was too thin, and because of a shortage of plasma. Finally, a date was chosen for the surgery. It was to be January 2.

As Mom's surgery was delayed and mine drew closer, I got a little anxious. Up to this point I had depended on the Lord to work everything out, so I didn't think this time should be any different. I decided to rest in the fact that God knows and loves us. That is all we need to understand. That is the faith part, which is our responsibility.

CHAPTER 9

It's Time to Go

The time came for my mother's surgery. It was hard to release her to the surgical technician. The staff had been kind to her up to that point, and I had no reason to think things would be any different after she left the room. Still, I felt like a mother handing over her child. Our roles had been reversed.

Mom was back with me in the room within forty-five minutes, and they said she did very well. My sister and I took turns staying with her a couple of nights. Mom never complained the first time about the discomfort of the surgery or the placement of that feeding tube.

A few days later the head nurse at the care center called me with concerns about Mom's temperature and respiration level. Her temperature was high and her respiration level was very low. The nurse said that Mom's attendants would monitor her closely and that if she didn't improve, they would have to send her to the hospital, which was a few streets away.

I told the nurse to keep me updated on Mom's status. A few hours later the phone rang and my heart dropped. I knew it was about Mom. The nurse said they were preparing to take her to the hospital. I told her I was on my way, called everyone who needed to know about the situation, and then headed to the hospital.

I got that call on January 9. Yes, it was that close to my surgery date. I didn't know what this was going to look like, but I was about to find out.

In the hospital ER, my mother's temperature continued to

spike. Her blood pressure and blood gas levels were low. The doctor ordered tests on her blood and took X-rays. After a couple of hours they still did not know exactly what was wrong and decided she needed to be admitted to the hospital from the ER.

My sister, Brenda and I and other family members were there, and we kept my brother, David, updated by phone since he lived in another state. We made many calls during those first few hours.

I took turns with Brenda staying with Mom. She was feverishly ill. When all of the test results arrived, the doctor's suspicions were confirmed. My mother had MRSA in both lungs. It was no wonder that her breathing was labored and that she had to be on high oxygen. I listened closely to her. Sometimes she didn't know she was in the world, but at other times I felt she knew exactly what was happening.

I would talk to her and she would just look at me. Mom couldn't see well, but I sometimes felt she was looking me straight in the eye. Every time my sister arrived and I would head home to rest, I hated leaving.

My surgery date was fast approaching. I was terribly torn. I didn't want to leave Mom, but I knew I had to have my surgery. I had prepared so long for this time. I did not know what God was doing, but I knew I had to trust Him. This didn't seem like a good plan to me, but did I know better than the Creator of the universe?

After spending many nerve-racking hours in a germ-filled hospital, my immune system was shot. I woke up on January 12 and I was sick. I was coughing and felt horrible. I thought, *Oh no! I can't be sick. Mom needs me. I have to have surgery, and the surgeon will not do it if I am sick. What am I going to do?*

I called to tell my sister I was sick, and Brenda told me not to come to the hospital. She knew I needed to get well for the surgery. Because Mom's immune system was compromised, it would not be wise for me to visit her while I was sick, so I monitored her status by phone. There was no change.

Brenda shared one bright spot. Mom had given her the prettiest smile in the early morning hours. That brought tears to my eyes. My mother was on her deathbed, and I knew it. My Facebook entries for the next couple of days read:

January 13, 2013

Joshua 24:7(MSG): "Then they cried out for help to God."

Judges 6:6(NIV) "Cried out to God for help."

Psalm 3:8(MSG): "Real help comes from God."

Psalm 34:17-18(MSG): "Is anyone crying for help? God is listening, ready to rescue you. If your heart is broken, you'll find God right there; if you're kicked in the gut, He'll help you catch your breath."

I know where my help comes from, and I have cried out for it today especially. My mother lies dying. I am sick and need to have my surgery in three days. It sounds hopeless, but I know God works when we can't see it.

I know everything works to the good for those whose Father is God. My heart is broken. There's nothing like the feeling of knowing your number-one fan (besides Jesus), your cheerleader in life, and the one who loves you no matter what, is leaving this earth. I know where my help and my hope come from, and I am letting Him carry me. I won't make it any other way.

January 14, 2013

Psalm 46:1–10(KJV):

> "God is our refuge and strength, a very present help in trouble. Therefore we will not fear, even though the earth be removed, and though the mountains be carried into the midst of the sea; though its waters roar and be troubled, though the mountains shake with its swelling. Selah
>
> There is a river whose streams shall make glad the city of God, the holy place of the tabernacle of the Most High. God is in the midst of her, she shall not be moved; God shall help her, just at the break of dawn. The nations raged, the kingdoms were moved; He uttered His voice, the earth melted. The Lord of hosts is with us; the God of Jacob is our refuge. Selah
>
> Come, behold the works of the Lord, who has made desolations in the earth. He makes wars cease to the end of the earth; He breaks the bow and cuts the spear in two; He burns the chariot in the fire. Be still, and know that I am God."

January 15, 2013

The Lord is not working things out; He has worked things out. On the eve of my first scheduled surgery, I have many emotions. The one that outweighs them all is thankfulness. In the midst of the commotion, the chaos, and the stormy winds of life, Jesus has spoken loudly, "Peace; be still." I told my family if I am headed for Nashville and Mom passes away, I do not want to be told until Friday after I finish my surgeries and am in recovery. The only thing I want to dwell on is that the

Lord has worked all things out. And when God does that, it is always for the good. In that I am resting.

> "There's within my heart a melody
> Jesus whispers sweet and low.
> 'Fear not. I am with thee. Peace; be still
> In all of life's ebb and flow.'
> Though sometimes He leads through waters deep,
> Trials fall across the way;
> Though sometimes the path seems rough and steep,
> See His footprints all the way.
> Jesus, Jesus, Jesus,
> Sweetest name I know,
> Fills my every longing,
> Keeps me singing as I go."

I planned to go on as scheduled. My health was better the morning of January 15. I had not so much as a cough. I went to the hospital to spend a little time with Mom before leaving for Nashville. I got in the bed with her and sang the song she always loved to hear me sing at the piano, "The King Is Coming." It was an emotional moment because the song was more real for her than ever before.

I received extra strength from the Lord to be able to sing that hymn without breaking down. I stroked Mom's hair. She loved it when I did that. I talked to her about old times and said anything else that came to mind.

The time arrived for me to go. I kissed Mom, told her goodbye, and said we would see each other again. I told her I loved her and thanked her for being a wonderful mother. A single tear ran down her face. I kissed her once more and left. I cried because I knew in my heart of hearts that this would be the last time I would see my mother on this side of heaven, and I was heartbroken.

I did in fact tell my family not to call me if Mom passed after I headed for Nashville. I wanted one thing only to be on my mind going into surgery. God had worked everything out. I truly believed that.

Proverbs 16:1-9(MSG) reads:

"Mortals make elaborate plans, but God has the last word. Humans are satisfied with whatever looks good; God probes for what *is* good. Put God in charge of your work, then what you've planned will take place. God made everything with a place and purpose; even the wicked are included—but for judgment. God can't stomach arrogance or pretense; believe me, he'll put those upstarts in their place.

Guilt is banished through love and truth; Fear-of-God deflects evil. When God approves of your life, even your enemies will end up shaking your hand. Far better to be right and poor than to be wrong and rich. We plan the way we want to live, but only God makes us able to live it."

God is faithful. He works things out and brings us where we need to be. He worked this point of time out for me. I did not know that He had done this down to the smallest detail, but I was soon to find out.

CHAPTER 10

Stay Positive

I left the hospital after saying good-bye to my mother and started for home, crying all the way. My heart was broken, but I had to give that to the Lord just as I had done with everything up to this point.

It was snowing and the road was starting to ice. I thought, *Boy, something or someone does not want me to get to Nashville*, and this made me more determined to go.

The Evil One will put obstacles in the way every time he thinks something good is going to happen. He doesn't want God to get any glory and works to tear down whatever points to God's goodness.

Travis, our son, was riding with Jerry and me to Nashville, and we were going to meet Tara, our daughter, at a rest area just beyond the Tennessee border. We had about another thirty minutes' drive. Cheryl, our other daughter, had already arrived at our hotel. I was thankful we had found rooms so close to the hospital since I had to be there at six the next morning.

We waited for Tara in the rest area. This quaint place was different from any rest area I had ever seen. It had an open room that was decorated like someone's den with a big stone fireplace and rocking chairs.

The older gentleman who worked at the rest area was friendly and told us he was retired and was there only part time. He asked where we were going, and I told him I was scheduled for surgeries at Vanderbilt. He was sorry to hear that, but I said I would be all right. God had supplied everything I needed up to that point and would continue to do so. He mentioned that his wife had cancer. Things had not gone so well for her.

When you have cancer you find there is no shortage of stories about people who have been touched by it in some way.

Tara pulled up and entered the building. We said our hellos. The elderly gentleman wished us well, and we told him good-bye as we went on our way. I will stop on one of my return trips to try to see him again.

We drove into Nashville and found our hotel and Cheryl. The two girls took one of the rooms we had reserved, and Travis, Jerry, and I took the other.

We got something to eat, and then we needed to get ready for bed because we had to be at the hospital early. We were facing a big day the next morning and an even bigger one after that.

I didn't have to do much to prepare for the next morning. I couldn't wear makeup, and I planned to wear a jogging suit to the hospital, so I laid out my outfit and packed a small bag. I knew I would not need much since I would be in the ICU the whole five days of my stay.

We settled down and I made my last Facebook post for what I was sure would be at least a week. My family was going to keep everyone updated on my progress by using my wall.

I washed my face, read my Bible, and tried to calm down and sleep. My plan was to get up around four the next morning, read my Scripture, write one last post saying "This is it!," and get ready. I wanted to ease into the morning and to arrive early at the hospital.

Did I say early? The phone rang and it was our other son, Kevin, who had to work that day and was planning to come that night to be there for the longer surgery.

I answered my phone still quite groggy because I had slept so peacefully. A voice said, "Hi, Mom. What are you doing?"

Suddenly awake, I panicked and asked, "Kevin, what time is it?" He said, "Five-fifteen." I said, "Oh honey, I have got to go. We have slept in. I will call you later as soon as we get to the hospital. Love you. Bye."

It was like a scene in *Home Alone*. I leapt out of bed, shouting that we had overslept, and told the guys to get up and to call the girls in the next room. I raced to the bathroom—no reading, no posting, no quick bath. I just jumped into clothes, but I was determined to style my hair a bit, no matter what.

Jerry warmed up the car. We piled in and drove down the street. I was thankful we were only about four minutes from the hospital. We made it with a few minutes to spare.

I got checked in, and we were shown to a waiting room in the main lobby. We were now able to return Kevin's call to tell him we had made it to the hospital. Tara called Kevin and let me talk to him, because I had already given her my purse with my phone to keep for me.

We hadn't been sitting long when someone called my name and waited for me at the open door. All my family members followed since they would be waiting in another room while I was in surgery. I didn't have time to reflect on anything, because my family kept me busy talking and answering questions.

We went upstairs to a small waiting room. I didn't sit there long either. The next time I was called, I went by myself to get ready. The nurse assured Jerry and the kids that they could come back when I got settled.

I was not looking forward to the injection of blue dye used to help extract some of my lymph nodes. I had dreaded it from the first time I had heard about it.

I had read about the injections three and half months earlier on the Internet. There were three in all. The doctor called in a prescription for a numbing ointment so that I could have it filled and bring it with me. I was supposed to apply this liberally all over the area to numb myself an hour before the injections. The ointment is also used in tattoo shops if that tells you anything.

The nurse asked if I had applied the cream, and I told her I had. She asked when, and I said I had done it before arriving at the hospital. "Let's apply some more," she said. That did not reassure me. She spread it much more liberally than I had.

I would soon be taken to the X-ray room for the injections. I braced for this, but I knew I would be put to sleep for the next part. They wheeled me downstairs and got me settled on the table, and I prayed that the injections would not hurt too badly.

It turned out that installing a guide wire for my lumpectomies had hurt worse. I am not going to say the injections were a piece of cake, but they were not as bad as I had allowed myself to imagine.

The Evil One will build horrible illusions, but they are merely shadows and cannot harm us. We must not yield to our overworked imaginations. That is why Scripture tells us to set our minds on good things. We must think good thoughts, dream good dreams, and focus on the positive rather than the negative.

I was returned to the same room, and then my family got to join me, though not all at once. The girls came back first. Jerry and the kids were strong, but it was hard for them to put on a brave face. They comforted me, though. I hated the fact that I was causing them distress, fear, or worry of any kind. I was also troubled that they would have to wait in the hospital so many hours this day and especially the next.

I heard directions being given and movement in the hallway. A nurse said that they were coming for me soon and that I would get a shot to help me relax. Those shots always put me out immediately.

Tara told me that Kevin was just around the block. I was surprised because he wasn't supposed to come until that night. He had made quick arrangements and had raced all the way to Nashville to arrive before they took me back.

I told Tara if he didn't make it to tell him I knew he had gotten there. The nurse came in at that moment and said she had something to help me go to sleep. She gave me the shot, and as she was doing this Kevin appeared in the doorway. I saw him, smiled, and tried to wave. That was the last thing I remember until I was in recovery.

CHAPTER 11
The Waiting Game

I woke up to the reality that I had had a breast removed. Under all those thick, heavy bandages I knew there was nothing. I did not dwell on that for long. I was thankful that my family was near and that I was not in any pain. My room was semi-private, and no one was in the bed next to the door. I was thankful for that.

After I was fully awake, my family joined me in the room. Jerry, Travis, Kevin, Tara, and Cheryl were all by my side. Their faces were sympathetic, and they smiled just as I had remembered before I went to sleep. They were glad to see me and happy that I was awake.

A nurse asked if I was in any pain, and I said no. God has blessed me with a high tolerance for pain, and for that I am thankful. She wanted to give me something just the same, so I agreed.

I had never had a breast removed before and didn't know what to expect. Taking that narcotic was a big mistake. I do not throw up easily, but the hard medication and the chicken noodle soup did not sit well. I had thrown up maybe fifteen times in my fifty-two years, and that was one of them. After that, I said I didn't want anything but Tylenol. The nurse was amazed that I was not begging for pain medication.

My younger daughter, Cheryl, was in college and needed to get back to her studies. She hated to leave, but I understood and wanted her to return to school. She got emotional at the thought of leaving. I assured her that everything would be all right and that everyone would keep her updated during my surgery the next day. She waited as late as she could, kissed me good-bye, and left.

The others decided to leave shortly after Cheryl did. It was going to be a long day and everyone needed rest. I asked about my phone, but it remained in my purse in the trunk of the car. Jerry told me I didn't need it. Everyone would be trying to call or text, and I shouldn't have to deal with that. I agreed. I certainly wouldn't need my phone the next day.

I tried to settle in and was surprised that I wasn't hurting much. I know it was probably because of adrenaline and the "can't wait" feeling for the next morning. I didn't envy Jerry and the kids, who had about an eight-hour wait on their hands, not counting the preparation and recovery time, but I knew this was what I had been waiting for. Months of preparation had brought me to this time and place. God had graciously led me every step of the way. I had arrived and I was thankful.

I had taken Tylenol, and the nurse was still amazed that this was all I wanted. I told her about being blessed with a high tolerance for pain, and she thought that was wonderful.

I read a little of the Bible I found in the top drawer of my nightstand. I made sure that my family left my reading glasses. The older I get the more they become a part of me. I prayed and thanked the Lord for working everything out. I finished praying, drifted off quickly, and slept soundly.

About three in the morning, I was awakened by attendants placing a lady in the bed next to mine. They pulled my curtain, but I could tell this woman was in great pain. She shouted each time they moved any part of her. My heart broke for this lady, and I prayed for her and for everyone taking care of her. I don't know exactly what was wrong, but judging by the conversation, it was a complex situation.

I tried to go back to sleep and managed somehow. I was awakened by a big light that was turned on for the morning shift change. Night nurses were getting their replacements up to speed on what had been done with each patient.

I got up and headed for the bathroom, but I needed help because I was hooked up to an IV pole. The nurse asked if I wanted something a little stronger for pain, but I told her no and thanked her.

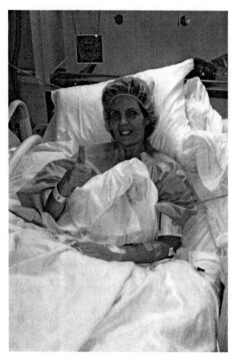

Here I am, sitting in a hospital bed and wearing a surgical cap.

I was elevated in bed when Jerry and the kids arrived. They looked somewhat rested, but I felt a little guilty about the day they were going to have. I repeated my request that they go as soon as I was taken into surgery, that they hunt the nearby mall and not miss any meals. I did not want them to feel they had to stay in a waiting room. They promised they would do as I asked, and for a little while, I wished I could go with them.

CHAPTER 12

A New Body

Ten o'clock arrived quickly, and I was about to be taken to another floor to be prepared for surgery. My family members kissed me, and I told them I would see everyone soon. The nurse put something in my IV that she said would make me sleepy, and I went out immediately. I don't remember anything after that until I woke up in the ICU.

My family told me it took quite a while for the surgery to start. A conflict in scheduling for the operating room led to a delay, and my family was called around noon when the surgery began. Jerry told me he and the kids indeed went to a mall and didn't miss any meals but still stayed a long time in the waiting room.

They told me of a little girl, not much older than six, who entertained them as my surgery was winding down. It ended about eight o'clock. They said my doctor spoke with them after the eight-hour operation and gave them the good news that it was a success. He said that I was the perfect candidate for this type of surgery and that I would be very pleased with the results. I still am today.

I don't know too much about the details of my surgery or how a surgical team does this type of operation. I was careful not to watch a YouTube video or anything else that showed how it was done. Reading about it was enough for me, and I decided to leave everything up to the doctor, his team, and the Lord.

I know the operation was like a transplant. One area of tissue was moved to another with an artery to feed it. I was cut from hip to hip, and then tissue was cut away. The surgeon took an artery, moved it to my chest along with the tissue, formed it into a breast, and hooked all the blood vessels together. It is amazing what excellent surgeons can accomplish.

A highly skilled hand was needed to cut away and to reconnect everything the right way. Through this surgery I received a new breast, which is 100 percent me, a new stomach, and a new naval. A tummy tuck was a perk of this operation.

Three drains were put in place—two from my lower abdomen and one coming from the side of my new right breast.

I don't remember recovery, but I do recall waking up in the ICU room where I would stay for four nights. I dimly remember someone saying that a penlike instrument had been placed in my hand and that if I needed something for pain I should push it. Not knowing what I was doing, I pushed it. Boy, did I regret that.

Remember, I don't do well on hard medicine, something all who were caring for me found out pretty quickly. I had nothing in my stomach, so I suffered dry heaves, which did not feel good. I told the attending nurse, "Get this thing away from me." I then repeated what I had told the nurse the previous day, that I wanted only Tylenol for pain control. She said that would not be strong enough, but I assured her it would.

Jerry and the kids came to visit, and I was glad to see them. It was late and dark outside. I asked if they were tired and said I wanted them to get some sleep. Travis said he would stay with me. I was thankful that it was a private room and that he would be there. It was a great comfort to know he was in the room with me. I did not want to wake him for anything, but knowing he was there in case I needed him was huge for me.

I could sleep in only one position—on my back with the bed elevated. I had practiced this position for several weeks since I knew it was the only way I would be able to sleep for a while.

With all the drains, the catheter, the IV, the heart monitor, and leg compressors, I was pretty much trapped in that bed. I felt like I had been hit by a Mack truck. I did not know that I would be monitored every hour on the hour with a Doppler. The hospital staffers had to make sure there was a constant blood flow to the new breast. If they did not hear the steady flow, something was wrong. It became music to my ears. I got to see my new breast right away, because they had to cover it loosely to make easy access for the hourly Doppler check.

I was told that the flap had a great color almost instantly. The warmth of the flap was also quite encouraging. I would soon be the talk of that department because this surgery was such a success. For the next forty-eight hours the staff checked and checked again.

Those irritating drains and the catheter were the only things that caused me discomfort. The drains were stitched into place at the points of entry, and when they got yanked, I felt every bit of it.

I also had to wear an abdominal binder, which gave me support where I had been cut from hip to hip to remove the flap. The binder kept riding up, and I tried to pull on it the best I could so it would not rub the surgery site.

The nurses attending to me were amazed that I took only Tylenol for pain. I told them each time how good God was. They told me what a good patient I was. I just gave them a smile and gave God the glory. He did it. He made a way and had everything worked out. All the details were planned, and He brought me to the surgery and through it. I am forever grateful.

CHAPTER 13

One Step at a Time

The next morning, Travis woke up and the rest of the family arrived at the hospital. I knew I was a sight by the light of day, but the hard part was over and I was on the mend. I knew my recovery would take a few weeks, but I was determined. I didn't feel like walking that first day, because my legs felt like rubber and would not hold me up.

For two days, my routine remained the same. I was checked around the clock with the Doppler, I received Tylenol and other medication, my drains were emptied, and tried to sleep despite everything that was hooked up to me.

A steady stream of nurses, doctors, and interns came in and out of the room. Some had heard what a success my surgery was, and they wanted to have a look. I got used to people taking a peek at the new part of my body.

I was thrilled that I was considered a success and was said to be so ahead of schedule for recovery. Again, I cannot stress enough my praise to God for it all. He has put me back together in the most awesome way. I am so thankful He found me worthy to be used to show what a wonderful God He is. I had asked only one thing throughout this journey, and that was for Him to show His strength. I wanted Him to still certain mouths and to let anyone looking on be awestruck by the great and powerful God whom I serve. That was exactly what was happening.

Tara had to get back to her family, and because of work, Travis was going to ride back with her part of the way to Bowling Green,

Kentucky. Shaunna, Travis's wife, would meet them there to pick up Travis. Jerry and Kevin would remain in Nashville.

Jerry at first had planned to stay in Nashville from that Tuesday to Thursday and then go home with Tara and travel back and forth from her place since it was only a two-hour drive versus the three-and-a-half-hour drive from home.

He instead decided to stay in Nashville with me, but he had to find another hotel because the one where he and Kevin were staying was booked up. They ended up next door at the sister hotel of the first place. Thankfully it was still only a few minutes from the hospital. They could have walked if it wasn't so cold.

The nurses removed the catheter, for which I was very grateful, but this meant it was time for me to get out of bed. I was instructed to walk in a hunchback position to avoid stretching my middle. I said this would not be a problem because I would do it automatically anyway. I had to call each time I got up, because I had to be unhooked from everything, especially the heart monitor and the leg compressors.

Moving with the three drains was a challenge. I had to make sure they did not hook on anything. I was praying to have them removed before leaving the hospital, since I was not draining very much. This impressed the staff.

Tara returned to the hospital the next day. She walked alongside of me as I ventured down the hall for the first time. I was excited to get out of the room. I walked like an old lady who had spine problems. When I stretched too much, I could feel a twinge in my abdomen, so I would bend more at the middle. I made three trips down the hall, and I was ready to get back in the bed. The surgery took a lot out of me, but the smiles of the nurses told me I was doing well in my recovery.

Kevin had to leave to get back to his family, but he didn't want to go. He planned to bring his family back the next day, but Jerry told him we would be home sometime on Monday and it wouldn't be necessary for him to make another trip.

Jerry had returned my phone to me. I told Kevin that I would call him and that he could call me. He felt better about leaving me then.

That Friday I learned of Mom's passing. Jerry was sitting with me, and a surgeon associate came in to check on me. She asked me how I was feeling. When she left the room, Jerry told me he would be right back.

I could hear a conversation in low tones, and when Jerry returned, the surgeon came with him. Jerry drew near the bed. I braced myself because I was fairly sure about what was coming. Jerry told me that "Georgie has a new address," and I knew exactly what he was saying. I was not shocked, but I started crying softly.

I didn't feel overwhelming grief because there was joy too. No one wants to be told his or her mother has died. Knowing I would have to find a new normal after so many years of the previous one was sad. I was sad for me, but oh no, not for her. I was so happy that she would not have to be in a bed suffering anymore. She was free and home.

The doctor asked if I wanted something to help me rest, and I again said no. I thanked her for her concern but told her I would be fine. She left and Jerry stayed for a little while before he also left.

I would not allow myself to dwell on the negative. I had too much to be grateful for. Anytime I found my mind wandering into the negative, I pictured my mother healthy, happy, and whole.

CHAPTER 14

Going Home

My cousin Theresa, who has lived in Nashville for years, came by with her husband for a visit the next day. I was so glad to see them. She brought a little devotion book to give me something to read while I lay in bed.

When Jerry and Tara left for the evening to return to the hotel, I decided to read a little of that devotion book. The first line I found said, "God's timing is always on time." Boy, was that spot on. I let myself wonder a little about my mother. I didn't do that too much unless it was to picture her finally in heaven with Daddy and getting to see Jesus, whom she loved. I couldn't allow my emotions to hinder my recovery.

Everything was taken care of, and I had to rest in that fact. God was in the details. I thought about that Wednesday morning when I had overslept. I had to rush to get ready to be at the hospital. Mom had passed around two-thirty that morning. If I had gotten up, eased into the morning, and done everything I had planned to do, I would have learned something that I had asked my family not to tell me and did not need to know as I prepared to go into surgery.

My family members deserve a lot of credit for that. They never once let on that anything was wrong and certainly not that my mother, their mother-in-law and grandmother, had left this world. My heart aches sometimes to know what they spared me during their hurt. I now understood why my youngest cried so much and had a hard time leaving me when returning to school.

She was also crying for me because of something I did not know at the time.

If I had signed in on Facebook, the first thing I would have seen was "RIP Mamaw Cox," written by my niece. God did not allow me to do that. He knew I had wanted to go into surgery thinking, *God has worked everything out,* and He had!

My God is so personal that He cares about things like that. There is nothing so large or so small that we cannot expect Him to deal with it, to work it out, or to answer us. He cares about the desires of our hearts. We have just got to love, to have faith, and to trust Him.

"For I know the plans I have for you, says the Lord, plans for welfare and not for calamity to give you a future and a hope" (Jeremiah 29:11 NIV).

We must believe that with everything in us. We have no hope outside of Christ Jesus.

My surgeons came each day, and both were ecstatic about the way I looked and about the status of my recovery. I was able to raise my right arm over my head. Having lymph nodes removed causes tightness and pain, so some patients have to do therapy and exercises to recover their mobility. I had been able to raise my arm since the first night. I had checked after I was fully awake. It was the first thing I consciously did. Those caring for me were amazed at how I had surpassed everything they wanted to see from me before I went home.

I was known as the perfect patient. I told them this had nothing to do with me. They also could not believe that although I was told my mother had passed away the morning of my first surgery I wasn't an emotional mess.

I told them how long my mother had been in a hospital bed and about the suffering that kept her there. "How could I be anything but happy for her?" I said. I told them how much I loved her and said that I would surely miss her but that it was her time.

She knew it and I knew it. I trusted in God to take care of me and my mother. My mother was perfect now.

Sunday rolled around, and it was time for Tara to leave. I was so thankful that my children could be with me. We all got to be together at one point. I didn't like the reason, but I was thankful for the togetherness felt.

Jerry and I were the only ones left in Nashville. Knowing I might go home the next day, I was happy. I was sitting more and more in a recliner-style chair. I was still wrestling with those drains, looking forward to the day when they would be gone for good. Their removal couldn't come soon enough for me.

I had put on makeup during the last two days of my stay and was looking and feeling more like myself, even if my hair was dirty. I knew when I got home that everything, even what I was going to wear, would be a challenge. I had no idea in the previous months how much space three drains took up on a person's body and the creativity it would take to dress with them.

Jerry brought me a cheeseburger for dinner that evening. It was so good. I didn't have much of an appetite the first few days after surgery. I was now able to unhook myself to make a trip to the bathroom without assistance, although I continued to walk with a humpback, bent-over posture.

I was still taking Tylenol but not for any pain in my surgery sites. I felt pain in the three places where the drains were stitched into my skin. The drains were very uncomfortable. I planned to tape them to me when I got home so they would not dangle so much.

Jerry left me that night, and I told him I would call as soon as someone told me I could go home. I slept pretty well even with the drains, the elevated bed, and the forced position on my back. I got up the next morning as usual, went to the bathroom, and got in my chair.

My doctor came in and said I would be released when all the

paperwork was finished. I was so happy to hear those words. I thanked him for everything. I couldn't say often enough what a blessing it was to have found him and what a blessing he was. He is a wonderful surgeon, and I greatly appreciated his work on me. He told me that my follow-up appointments would be scheduled so they would fall on the same day as the appointments with my other surgeon. They have always been great about that, and I especially appreciate it when I have to travel any distance to see them.

I called Jerry and then the kids to tell them the news that I was coming home. Jerry arrived about an hour later after having breakfast. I knew I wouldn't have to do much. I was going to wear what I wore entering the hospital, but I knew that because of the drains, getting into my clothes would be a tight squeeze.

A nurse came by to let me know I could go anytime I was ready. After five days in that room, I was definitely ready to go home to be surrounded by my family and to rest where a person can rest best.

She went over instructions and things I should be aware of. My body had been rearranged, and a lot of problems could occur with my reconstruction. They could be extra troublesome since I was three hours away from my surgeon.

I asked her for my appointment date, and my heart sank a little. I would have to wait one week and a day to say good-bye to my drains, but I was going home!

CHAPTER 15

Good News, Great God

I got dressed and felt like I was crammed into my clothes. I looked comical. There I was in my sweat suit, stuffed full of me and my drains, walking like an old woman. I didn't put on my coat because I knew it would be impossible to get it off once I got positioned in the car.

Jerry left to warm up the car because it was about twenty degrees outside and felt even colder with the wind chill factored in. I said my good-byes and thanked the hospital staffers for the wonderful care they had given me during my six-day stay. They were kind and considerate.

They told me one last time that I was their perfect patient, and I once again told them who was perfect and said I was well because of Him and His grace.

An attendant wheeled me down to the lobby where we waited for Jerry to pull up to the front of the hospital. It was cold even inside because the doors were opened and closed so often. Jerry arrived with the car, and I told the attendant my ride was here. I thought, *Well, here we go.* After I got in the car and settled myself, we headed for London—home, sweet home. I smiled. I couldn't believe it. The searching, researching, planning, appointments, meetings, testing, and everything else were all over. I had had my surgery, and now I was headed home.

We stopped in Bowling Green, Kentucky, to get a bite to eat. I laughed at the thought of appearing in public looking the way I looked and wondered what people would think of me.

We found one of our favorite places, Chick-fil-A, and Jerry went in to get something for us. I did really well on the trip but got a little tired closer to London. Some of the kids and the grandkids were there to welcome us home.

I slowly made my way inside with help and positioned myself in our recliner, which would be my bed for the next three weeks. Getting up and down was not easy, and I needed help each time. The day when I could reach down and throw the handle to the recliner, I knew I was getting stronger and was well on my way to full recovery.

That evening, having been home only six and a half hours, I received a call from the surgeon who had done my mastectomy. Jerry took the call and handed me the phone. I said hello, and she told me that she had come by my hospital room and was sorry she had missed me. She said she had some news that she thought I would like to know and that she wanted to tell me herself.

The surgeon said she had received my official pathology report and was happy to report that no cancer could be found in the lymph nodes that were taken or in the breast tissue itself. I was ecstatic and she was too.

I thanked her for her skill in surgery, for her care, and for calling and said I greatly appreciated her. I told her that God is so good. The surgeon said she was happy for me and wished me well. She told me she would see me at our post-op appointment the next week. I said I looked forward to it.

I wanted to jump out of the recliner. By the time I hung up the phone, my family knew something good had happened. I could not contain myself. I could hardly get the words out fast enough and recounted the whole conversation. Everyone was joyful and smiling.

I had to call people. I called family. I called our music minister, who had come to the hospital before the first lumpectomy took place and had called many times to check on us. I called our pastor. He had called and texted us and had had the church pray corporately for me before my surgery.

The news had spread like wildfire. When the pastor answered the phone, he said, "Well, there's the lady of the hour." I smiled and laughed because I knew he had already heard.

I reminded him of a sermon he had preached one Sunday. He had talked about the Israelites, who were up and down in their faith despite witnessing many examples of God's power. The examples included the cloud by day and the fire by night, manna falling from heaven, and the parting of the Red Sea.

The pastor told us he longed to see something like that. He said, "God, I would take a mud puddle parting." I immediately started to cry and asked God if I could be the pastor's mud puddle. I whispered a short, heartfelt prayer. I reminded my pastor of that message and of his wish and told him what I had prayed. "I am your mud puddle," I said. He laughed and said he would take that.

The pastor said he was happy for me and was amazed at my faith. I told him that my delivery from cancer was all God's work and that He had carried me most of the way. The pastor reminded me that I had let Him. We ended our conversation. I was smiling.

I was beside myself. I was overjoyed at the thought that everything was just as I had prayed and begged God for it to be. I still am overwhelmed by the news that no cancer was found in a part of my body where imaging and tests proved it to be.

I can't thank God enough for providing everything I needed when I needed it. I felt that my family and I and all who were watching were in this together and that we would see something that would bless everyone. We saw God move in a mighty way. I need to hold on to that as long as I can. We are frail humans, just like the Israelites, aren't we? We have short memories and easily forget the goodness of God.

CHAPTER 16

It's Not Good-bye

My two daughters-in-law, Kandis and Shaunna, became my personal nurses. They took turns emptying, measuring, and cleaning my drains and helped me with my bandages and with dressing. I was so thankful for these two natural nurses. Kandis has since started nursing school and is doing very well. I knew she would.

I rested the day after I got home, because my mother's funeral would take place the next day. I had purposely pushed away the thought the whole week prior, and now the day was almost here. I did not have a clue what I would wear.

I racked my brain and finally recalled a black dress hanging in my closet. I had bought it at a secondhand store a few years earlier. It was a straight, mid-length long-sleeved dress. By that time it was way too big on me. I had lost three dress sizes with my healthy eating and now even more because I had a less fleshy midriff after my surgery. I decided to try it anyway.

I had one of the girls wash my hair the night before. Tara had arranged for my hairdresser, Ashley, to come to the house to style my hair. I was thankful for the many people who had provided such an outpouring of love from the five months before my surgery up to that point. Their cards, messages, texts, visits, gifts, and prayers gave me great encouragement.

My faith family was awesome. One group had put together a basket full of everything I could possibly use during my recovery—a journal, pens, Kleenex, picture frames, lotion, a devotion book, even a squishy little pillow that became my best friend for leverage in lying down. A cream-color soft-velvet throw became a constant hug from my friend Kim. I will never forget the many acts of kindness toward me and my family.

As I was about to put on my dress, I prayed it would be adequate. It was perfect. It slipped over all the drains, and the bulge in my middle from the binding was hardly visible. I still had to walk slumped over, but I was learning how to make this look graceful. Ashley had done a remarkable job on my hair, and I was thankful. I looked in the mirror and was pleased with what I saw. Ashley would not let me pay her. She refused and said she was glad to help me. I wanted to look my best for Mother's life celebration.

We all made our way to Pineville, a forty-five-minute drive from London. I had butterflies in my stomach. The closer we got, the more nervous I felt. I didn't get to see my mother after her death, and this would be the first time I had done that. The funeral would make her death real, and I wanted to run away.

I had not allowed myself to grieve, and I didn't know what to expect. I told the Lord that He had gotten me through the last six months and that I was leaning on Him wholly this time too. I planned to sing the song I had sung to Mom in her hospital bed when I said good-bye. I had sung it perfectly without crying, but I wasn't sure I could do that again.

When we arrived Jerry came around to my side of the car to help me out. It was a bitterly cold day, but I was not able to hurry into the funeral home. I made my way up the ramp and through the front door.

My sister, Brenda, and her family were already there. My brother David, his wife, Kristi, and their family had also arrived. My brother Eddie, whom I had not seen for quite some time, was there too. I had pictured that day a few times since Mom had had her stroke, but not in great detail, and now this is what it looked like.

I made my way up to the casket. I had picked out a beautiful tan suit for Mom a few years before, and she was wearing it. She loved her crystal pink beads and pink rhinestone broach, and she was wearing them. She loved pink, and her casket was a soft pink. She looked beautiful. One of my granddaughters said, "She looks like a princess in a box," and she did.

For the first time in many years, my beautiful, sweet mother looked like she had before the stroke took her away and she became a shell of herself. I was so thankful. She would have been pleased in her humble way.

The funeral home directors were kind and had a big winged-back chair positioned in the front row for me. They knew what I had been through the past week and were accommodating. The word soon spread to all who were there that God had healed me, so when people approached me, each encounter became a joyous celebration.

It was both a happy and a sad time. The feeling was bittersweet. We all had mixed emotions. There were hugs for comfort and hugs of joy, often by the same person.

The service would soon start. I made my way to the piano to be ready since I was first on the program. I said a quick prayer to ask God for the strength to play and to sing for His glory in honor of my mother.

The preachers entered and took their seats behind me. When they were seated, the recorded music stopped and I struck the first chord on the piano. Once again I started singing my mother's favorite song, "The King Is Coming." Halfway through, I saw my sister get out of her seat and make her way to the casket. Brenda was with our mother when she passed. My sister was having a hard time with her grief. She leaned over, kissed Mom, and returned to her seat.

My voice seemed strong, and I played like I had done for years. I finished, stood up, and the reality of the event hit me. I broke down momentarily, and I don't know who came to take my arms and to return me to my seat.

I had asked a friend who has the most beautiful voice to sing a couple of songs when the time came for Mom's funeral. She sang those songs and I could feel peace.

A few years before, I also had asked a minister friend, who had been our pastor, including Mom's, to officiate at the funeral. He did a wonderful job, and again I felt peace.

If there is one word to describe those three hours, it is *peaceful*. This was so fitting for a woman who loved her God, her husband, her children, and all those she met down through the years. She was humble but was the strongest woman I have ever known or will know. She was a graceful and elegant lady and a Proverbs 31 woman, and I will miss her until the day I die.

The service ended and it was time to leave. As people passed by, I saw their tears and received their hugs. Then it was my turn to say good-bye. Jerry helped me lean over the casket to tell my "Mommie", "See you later." I kissed her, prayed, and thanked the Lord for such a wonderful mother.

We all gathered in the entry hall to get ready to leave for the forty-five-minute drive to the cemetery. I had planned to stay in the car because I remembered how careful the hospital staff was to keep the temperature in my room at a steady seventy-three degrees so my transplant would stay warm. When we arrived, however, I couldn't stay in the car with all of my family outside around my mother's casket.

I got out and Jerry helped me climb the little embankment up to the gravesite. My sister-in-law, Kristi, had a heavy lap throw and ran to get it out of her car. My other sister-in-law, Linda, got everyone to block the wind to keep it from reaching me. I felt the unity of our close-knit group and the peace of God so strongly. Unveiled love washed over me, and I was thankful.

We asked Brandon, my son-in-law, to say something at the graveside. His words were gracious and fit the moment perfectly. He had not gotten to know Mom as she was before her stroke and said he felt he knew her much better on this day. I was proud of him for his remarks.

My friend Kim, whose husband officiated at the service, and Linda helped me to the car. We were frozen by the sharp wind that whipped around us. They positioned me in the car, each giving me a hug, and then we headed home.

My heart was full of happiness and sadness at the same time. On the drive home I thought about the new normal without my mother on this earth. I didn't dare dwell on this for long, and I couldn't because the thought of my healing would bring a smile. I was for sure experiencing mixed emotions, with thankfulness always on my mind.

CHAPTER 17
Anxiously Counting the Days

A lot of thoughts were running through my head. Good memories I would allow; thinking of my new normal without Mom I would not. We got home and everyone followed us and gathered in our house. The group consisted of out-of-town family and those close by. It included all my kids, all my grandkids, my husband, my brother and his family, and my sister and her family. I think we had thirty-two altogether.

Our neighbors cooked us a meal and brought it to the house. It felt good to have everyone there. Mommy would have been so happy and would have enjoyed herself, but she was in a much better place. I felt a very strong love in our full house that evening.

I hung on to the thought that my mother was in a better place. The older folk used to say of those who had died, "They have outstripped us." I finally knew what that meant. Even now, when grief threatens to choke me, I picture Mom taking in the sights of heaven, seeing Jesus, and standing with Daddy, both of my parents whole and perfect. Yes, I am sad for me but so very happy for her. A child of God can say "See you later," and that is what I dwell on when I am thinking about Mom. Scripture tells us to focus on good things.

"Summing it all up, friends, I'd say you'll do best by filling your minds and meditating on things true, noble, reputable, authentic, compelling, gracious, the best, not the worst, the beautiful, not the ugly, things to praise, not things to curse. Put into practice what you learned from me, what you heard and saw and realized. Do that, and God, who makes everything work together, will work you into his most excellent harmonies" (Philippians 4:8 MSG).

We need to think about the positive. I can't think of anything more positive than a perfect God who so loves an imperfect person. We have a heavenly Father who loves His children unconditionally. If we know that, we can get through any trial.

That evening, as my family rallied around me and we sat in our living room, we reminisced about old times. Some were good and some not so good. We laughed at the antics Daddy would sometimes pull when he was drinking. Some of the things we recalled surprised the older grandkids, who did not know much about this man.

Dad became a Christian when they were small children, so they did not know the drinking Melvin Cox. We were thankful for the change we had seen in my father during the last ten years of his life. Whether he was a good or a bad influence, we were the products of knowing and loving that man, and we all appreciated that fact.

As evening continued on, more and more family members left. Some had to travel great distances and some down the road just a piece. I hated the reason for the gathering but loved the fact that we got to be together. We had not been with each other for so long. David and Kristi remained with us one more night.

My mind would wander from time to time, but my family kept me busy talking. I would smile and even laugh out loud at the thought of my healing and then wipe away a tear thinking of my mother. I would smile at the thought of something my mother did or said and then shed a tear of gratitude to the Lord for His merciful healing. I was riding a roller coaster of emotions, but it was all good. Life is good.

The next day, after my brother left, I decided to try to take a shower by myself. Jerry would be close by, so I knew I would have help if I needed it. I had rigged up a cloth belt and had tied it together at the ends. I had found some good ideas for dealing with drains more easily. Jerry and I had made a list of things I would need and had bought them in advance of my surgeries. They came in handy.

Jumbo safety pins were among the items on that list. I carefully took each drain bulb out of the pocket belt that Jerry and I had made and pinned each bulb to the cloth belt. I had to orchestrate the pinning so I would have enough room and would not pull them. I still had to take Tylenol for the irritation the drains produced. I was a sight with the drains dangling as I tried my best to wash around them and not to pull at the same time.

I feel for anyone who has to have drains. You can't understand the burden they create unless you have had them. I counted the days when I could go to Nashville to have them removed.

Trying to get dressed was another complex task. I unpinned each drain and removed the soaked cloth belt. I found it easier to lay each drain on the bed and had to make sure I was close enough to the bed so I would not pull them off. That would have hurt. I put on my drain belt and then placed each drain in its own pouch. I was then free to hunchback walk around the room to get my clothes.

I hated this procedure, but I knew I had to go through it to get through it. I couldn't wait for the day when the drains were removed.

The girls were still emptying, measuring, and what they called stripping the drains to clean them. I emptied them only half a dozen times, and I am so grateful to Kandis and Shaunna for their care during those nine days of waiting to have the drains taken out.

Nights were difficult as I struggled to get comfortable. I went through a ritual of adjusting the pillows, arranging the drains, pulling the covers, constantly yanking down the abdomen belt, and waking Jerry for bathroom runs.

Jerry slept on the couch and was only one step away from me. He insisted on staying in the living room with me, and I was very thankful for his help.

I couldn't have done this without him. God took care of that detail months before my surgeries. Jerry retired just weeks before I got the diagnosis, allowing him to be home so he could transport me to and from appointments and walk on this journey with me. He has served me as Christ served the church, His bride.

After several days I realized I would probably be dealing with numbness for the long term. I still can't feel anything across my new belly button and flat stomach or my new breast over to the middle of my chest. This annoys me at times, but I have gotten used to it.

I hated the fact that I could not pick up my grandchildren. They were so sweet about being careful around me. They were told not to "bump Granna," and they tried their best to avoid doing that. It warmed my heart when one of them would stand next to my chair and observe me. The older ones obviously wanted to ask questions but didn't know what or how to ask.

I tried to think on their level so I could figure out what they might want to know about how I looked or felt. At least the drains were good for something. They made good conversation pieces. As long as my grandchildren saw that I wasn't in pain, they were fine. It was wonderful to share God's goodness with them and to tell them that He took away my cancer. That brought smiles every time.

CHAPTER 18
Freedom to Laugh Out Loud

The day I had been waiting for finally arrived. We headed for Nashville for my post-op appointment. I was delirious at the thought of getting the three annoyances out of my life forever. I eagerly anticipated being drain-free, and I am sure everyone who had spent time with me the previous week felt the same way. I was very careful not to complain or to complain as little as possible. Still, I knew family and friends would be happy for me.

We got to Nashville, pulled into the parking lot, parked, and walked to the door. It was the most I had walked since my surgery, and I felt a little weak. I realized I had to build up some muscle and my strength but felt I was healing wonderfully. I knew my doctors would be glad to see me. I could honestly tell them the drains were the thing that had bothered me the most.

We made our way up the escalator, and I went to the desk to check in. Jerry and I waited until I was called to go to the exam room. As we sat there, I couldn't help watching the people who passed by. Many were in different stages of cancer. Some wore turbans because their hair had fallen out from chemotherapy.

One woman wore a look saying she had just been told that doctors had found something. My heart broke for her because I knew exactly the journey she was beginning. I wanted to run after her, if I could have run, to tell her there was hope. I wanted to scream to all of them, "There's hope!"

My name was called and I snapped back to reality. Jerry and I made our way to the nurse and the open door. We walked down the hallway, and both my doctors were waiting for me. I had separate appointments, but they decided to see me together.

I still was considered a healing success with a remarkable recovery time. They couldn't believe that I was able to climb up on the table by myself. I told them I had been pulling the arm on the side of the recliner for a couple of days, which was a benchmark for me.

My mastectomy surgeon bragged on the work my plastic surgeon had done. They couldn't believe that I was taking only an occasional Tylenol. They asked if I was having any problems, and I told them about the troublesome drains. One of my doctors said she could take care of that.

I was prepared to have them extracted. I steadied myself because I was sure the drains would inflict a parting shot of pain. To my surprise, they didn't hurt that badly, or maybe I was so ecstatic about having them removed that I felt little discomfort. Either way, they were gone! I felt free. I thought I could jump, but I didn't. My surgeons and the nurse were all smiles, and it felt like a celebration.

I thanked my surgeons and again told them how much they were appreciated. I felt God had led me to them and had used them as tools in His hands as they used their scalpels in theirs. The Lord had a plan and worked it to perfection.

I felt so much smaller and lighter. I was eager to get on with my recovery, and I felt I had just gotten a big jump on it.

I would sleep in my bed/recliner for the next two weeks. My sleep did not return to normal for quite a while. I have always been a side sleeper, and I could not sleep on my right side. I couldn't put weight on that side of my chest or on the arm from which three lymph nodes had been taken. If I slept on my left side too long, however, gravity pulled at my right side.

My best position seemed to be lying on my back with pillows propping up limbs here and there. I also had to put something under the pillow to help support my head on the side to which I turned. Sleep has been different for me since the surgery, but fortunately I can sleep on my left side now.

I looked forward to returning to my active life with a new, slimmer me. I had lost all the fat that I had anywhere. All my clothes either swallowed me or fit better than ever before. Well-meaning people told me I needed to put on weight.

In my mind, I would say, *No I don't*. I was determined to eat as healthily as possible. I was a sugar addict and I knew it. I wasn't going back there. I have gained about ten pounds in the year since my surgery and feel for the most part that they are healthy pounds. For my height, my weight is just about right. Like everyone else, I struggle to make healthy choices about food. Doing this has involved a lifestyle change and an overhaul in my thinking about what is healthy.

I come into contact with many people, and the conversation always turns to what I am most passionate about: loving Jesus, being healthy, and spending time with my grandchildren.

These encounters always end with people giving me their email addresses after I have promised to send them the research that I did for myself. Many people have encouraged me to write a book on the subject and on my experience, so here it is. My story is Christ's story. I would not have this testimony of love, healing, and wholeness if it had not been for Jesus.

CHAPTER 19

Where Love Is

It has been a few years since my first post-op appointment. Looking back on my journey, I am still amazed at what the Lord brought me through. I am in awe of Him and of how He orchestrated every little detail.

He did it for me and He will do it for you. Believe that. His love is amazing and His peace is abundant. It is ever present and available to you.

It is often said that, "Home is where the heart is." Home is a place where you feel loved and find peace. It's a place where you long to be and most often want to stay.

"For where your treasure is, there your heart will be also" (Matthew 6:21 KJV).

Home seemed to be a theme in my six months of dealing with cancer. I read about it, saw mottoes, read signs, and even adopted a song with the title "Home" as my theme song, my marching song. When I hear it played over the radio or over a loudspeaker in a store, I lovingly listen and feel every emotion that comes with it.

"Settle down; it'll all be clear.
Don't pay no mind to the demons; they fill you with fear.
The trouble it might drag you down.
If you get lost, you can always be found.
Just know you're not alone,
'Cause I'm gonna make this place your home."

I felt like the Lord was speaking to me personally every time I listened to this song. Where is my home? For the child of God, it is in heaven, but I feel I am there now in a sense. A child of God is already a kingdom citizen.

"Those who live in the shelter of the Most High will find rest in the shadow of the Almighty. This I declare about the Lord, He alone is my refuge, my place of safety. He is my God, and I trust Him" (Psalm 91:1-2 NLT).

Our home as God's children is Him and His love. Wherever we are, we are home if we love and trust Him. His love is our home. He is our home. Home is a place to which we can always run and where we can feel safe. We can find unconditional love and acceptance there.

No matter what we face, our Father loves us and is there for us. He rushes to our rescue when we face obstacles and threats. We can enter His presence anytime because of the adoption made possible by Jesus. He places our feet on solid ground even when the earth seems to be shaking under us.

God has given me that wide open space, and I am overwhelmed by His love. I praise Him for His continued mercy and grace in my life. I still am amazed and thankful for what God has done, is doing, and will do in my life for His glory.

"I'm thanking God, Who makes things right. I'm singing the fame of heaven-high God" (Psalm 7:17 MSG).

God calls those still wayward and roaming. He invites those who are lost in the cares of this world, running around seemingly with no hope. He bids the weary who are tired and want rest to come.

It is a wonderful thing when you have been on a journey and find yourself headed down a familiar road. The closer you get to home, the more you feel that you cannot get there fast enough.

What a blessing to hear those words that make the longing go away. You are approaching a peace that brings promised rest, comfort, and tranquility. "Welcome home" is a wonderful greeting to hear from someone who loves you.

Each time I am honored to tell my story, I rejoice to know that the Father is being lifted up. This is all I ever wanted or asked for during my journey through cancer. I knew the Lord would take care of everything else. God has done a miracle. It is on full display, and He says, "Look and see." I am overwhelmed by His loving care in every little detail during this time in my life.

Dear hearts, never give up or allow yourselves to be counted out, because we have a Father who loves us and is always looking out for our good. Is holding on to faith during trials hard to do? Yes, but it is a must for the child of God.

I never would have chosen this journey for myself, but I thank the Lord for the things I learned on it. I had sweet fellowship with others, gained understanding along the way, experienced a great miracle in my life, and was given the honor of sharing this witness with others.

There is joy in the journey through cancer. I have experienced it for myself. I am forever touched and have a tender heart when I hear of someone who has just been given this life-changing diagnosis.

Such people must understand that they are not alone but have someone who will be with them even in those closed-in places that make them feel they are being suffocated.

God loves you. I encourage you to rest in the peace of that love. Feel very much at home in His love. He has a plan for your life. Trust that. Trust Him.

AFTERWORD

What follows this paragraph is an e-mail that I send whenever people request more information. I meet these people at work, in the supermarket, at church, and in other places. I wish someone had done this research and shared it with me when I was diagnosed with cancer. In no way am I suggesting treatment or offering medical advice. I am not a doctor or even a medical adviser. However, this self-education and research led me to good health. My prayer is that anyone who reads this document may also enjoy good health.

I am offering a lot of information.

Just before my cancer eight and a half years ago, I started reading, researching, and finding out how herbs work to heal and to keep the body well. I am still learning. PH level is one of the most important factors. It must be seven or a little above that number.

Good eating habits are essential. Fruits and vegetables are key. Vitamins and nutrient supplements are important. Detoxing is important. We are bombarded by chemicals all around us. Our immune systems cannot work the way God intended if they are bogged down and overloaded. Do what you can do and trust God for the rest.

Everything cells need for vitality works together in harmony and perfect balance when obtained from a healthy whole food diet and whole food supplements. If you have a weak immune system, find out what is out of balance and lacking in your body.

Natural lifestyle centers see major improvements in bloodwork, symptoms, and vitality in only a week or two mainly with these steps. Aluminum-free baking soda is a must to keep your body alkaline neutral. Use aluminum free, because aluminum is bad for the human body. This is a good place to start. You can put a quarter teaspoon in a glass of water (spring or distilled, gallon jug, no bottles). You need not do this all the time, just when you feel a little out of balance. The more you keep your body clean, the more you will recognize when your pH is out of balance.

Eliminate sugar. Believe me, that is hard. Once your body is cleansed (void of toxins, bad bacteria, viruses, and renegade cells) and deficiencies are corrected, you have the foundation that will maintain your health and a strong immune system. You must immediately go on a strict diet of nothing but raw vegetables, fruit, and water for at least a week. Get fresh baby spinach. It will seem like you are eating leaves, but do it. No pop, no sugar. Get some baking soda (aluminum free), put a quarter teaspoon in water, and drink the full glass. Sip on it if you have to. Do that one time a day.

Vitamins, nutrients, and minerals and what they're needed for:

A- (beta-carotene) eye and liver health; boosts immune system

B12- energy, nervous system health, red blood cells that carry oxygen through the body

C- immune system; supports vascular system, strong bones

D- stimulates immune system; works with calcium and magnesium; supports strong bones.

It's been discovered that people lacking in vitamin D have more upper respiratory illnesses than those with sufficient vitamin D.

E- breathing, brain function, wound healing, skin and liver health

Curcumin- high antioxidant, cancer fighter, supports skin, memory, heart, joints; is the spice turmeric and a blood thinner, anti-inflammatory, anticancer, antitumor; helps prevent cancer metastasis

Magnesuim- heart, nerves, bone building; works with calcium; helps good night sleep

Resveratrol- heart health, prevents blood clots and supports healthy blood vessels

CoQ10- heart, immune system, liver, kidney; high antioxidant

Grape seed extract- circulation; high antioxidant

Kelp- cell function; purifies the body, thyroid health; reduces blood clots

MSM- reduces inflammation; high antioxidant to detox chemicals from the body

A lack of magnesium can cause many problems, such as an inability to sleep.

Magnesium supports proper brain, nerve, lung, and digestive function. Magnesium and calcium make for better nerve function. This will ensure that the correct messages are sent to all your organs, glands, and muscles so they can function properly.

Flaxseed oil: This oil helps reduce tumor growth and is comparable to tamoxifen without the side effects. It also helps clear the bowels for elimination of toxins and reduces inflammation.

Dark greens: Your liver loves dark green vegetables. (It hates sweets and fats.) They help fight cancer, promote bone growth, clean your liver, and are filled with antioxidants.

Cruciferous vegetables: Broccoli, cabbage, bok choy, cauliflower, salad radishes, mustard greens, turnips, rutabaga, kale, collard greens, and watercress are all cruciferous vegetables. After years of claiming that diet had no connection to cancer, the American Cancer Society finally began promoting cruciferous vegetables as a cancer preventative.

I get my vitamins, nutrients, and minerals at a natural-food store. I use the NOW brand.

Using a juicer can be a great help. The nutrients from juiced fruits and vegetables immediately enter your system instead of having to go through the digestive process.

A good juice to start with consists of three carrots and one apple or three carrots, two celery sticks, and half a cantaloupe. Stay away from caffeine, sugar, and other chemicals as much as possible. You must free your body of chemical buildup.

I know this seems like a lot, but if you do a little at a time it will make a difference. If you do what you can, you can be sure God will do the rest. You can trust Him.

A good detox for the body if health allows

I have found this routine is best for me.

First five days- Nothing but raw fruits and vegetables (as many as you want). When you are in the produce section of the store, look at all the choices. We normally stick to five or six. The greener the better.

You will feel like you are bored or dying of starvation by day three, but stick with it. If you absolutely must, use just the smallest amount of dressing to dip, not drown, your veggies.

Day six- Add cooked vegetables to your raw ones.

Day ten- Add fish or chicken to the evening meal.

By day fourteen (two weeks) you should see a big improvement in the way you feel, your energy level, and your sleep.

If you continue, in five weeks, you will be thirty pounds lighter. You will find that your metabolism has changed, and you will burn calories faster. If you do not need to lose the thirty pounds, trim the time down. The first week is a good detox within itself.

This is not easy by any means. You have to know why you are doing this and keep that in mind at all times. Ask the Lord to help you.

Drinking water when you feel hungry will help, and the urge to eat will pass. Your body has been conditioned to crave caffeine, sugar, and the chemicals in many of our foods. Eating out of a box, a bag, or a can promotes these addictions.

Our bodies were made for real food—food that was once alive and growing.

Do what you can do, and start where you can.

I have read, studied, and take turmeric. I use the powder form because turmeric will stain badly when you try to chip or cut the root.

Turmeric helps reduce the inflammation that causes so many problems in the human body.

I use a recipe published by Jim Kelmun. He called it his "homemade chemotherapy."

The recipe includes two ingredients: aluminum-free baking soda and 100 percent grade-B maple syrup.

I used it when I had cancer and was awaiting surgery. I also use it once or twice a year for cleansing.

Kelmun said the maple syrup targets cancer cells, which are said to consume fifteen times more glucose than normal cells do; the bad cells love sugar. The baking soda is pulled into the bad cells with the maple syrup.

The baking soda, being highly alkaline, is the main anticancer substance. The maple syrup is a carrier, allowing the baking soda to enter the cancer cells.

The recipe calls for one level teaspoon of baking soda and three level teaspoons of syrup.

Use a Pyrex pot or a stainless steel pan.

Stir the mixture briskly on low heat for five minutes. If the mixture tastes terrible, you have burned it, which is easy to do. But if you keep it just warm enough so that it doesn't burn, the two substances will combine and the taste will be quite pleasant.

You can take two teaspoons per day for a few days. I took mine for three days.

Read Scripture dealing with healing

Affliction will not rise up a second time! The Enemy will sometimes send a spirit of affliction to attack your body, your mind, and your productivity for the Lord. This is an assault sent from hell against workers in the kingdom of God. A friend came to my home to give me this same message while I was going through this trial of cancer. I have thought on this scripture and let it lift me up during that time in my life.

> The Lord is good, a stronghold in the day of trouble; and he knows them that trust in Him ... What do you imagine against the Lord? He will make an utter end: affliction shall not rise up the second time ...
>
> Thus says the Lord: "Though they be quiet and likewise many, yet thus shall they be cut down when he shall pass through. Though I have afflicted you, I will afflict you no more. For now I will break his yoke from off you, and will burst your bonds in sunder ... Behold, on the mountains the feet of him that brings good tidings, that publishes peace! ... For the wicked shall no more pass through you; he is utterly cut off." (Nahum 1:7, 9, 12-13, 15 KJV)

"My son, give attention to my words; incline your ear to my sayings. Do not let them depart from your eyes; keep them in the midst of your heart; for they are life to those who find them, and health to all their flesh. Keep your heart with all diligence, for out of it spring the issues of life" (Proverbs 4:20–23 NIV).

"Not a word failed of any good thing which the Lord had spoken to the house of Israel. All came to pass" (Joshua 21:45 NKJ).

"For it is God who works in you both to will and to do for His good pleasure" (Philippians 2:12 NKJ).

"But if the Spirit of Him who raised Jesus from the dead dwells in you, He who raised Christ from the dead will also give life to your mortal bodies through His Spirit who dwells in you" (Romans 8:11 NKJ).

"For all the promises of God in Him are Yes, and in Him Amen, to the glory of God through us" (2 Corinthians 1:20 NKJ).

"And behold, a leper came and worshiped Him, saying, 'Lord, if You are willing, You can make me clean.' Then Jesus put out His hand and touched him, saying, 'I am willing; be cleansed.' Immediately his leprosy was cleansed." (Matthew 8:2-3 NKJ).

"If you diligently heed the voice of the Lord your God and do what is right in His sight, give ear to His commandments and keep all His statutes, I will put none of the diseases on you which I have brought on the Egyptians. For I am the Lord who heals you." (Exodus 15:26 NKJ).

"So you shall serve the Lord your God, and He will bless your bread and your water. And I will take sickness away from the midst of you." (Exodus 23:25 KJV).

"And the Lord will take away from you all sickness, and will afflict you with none of the terrible diseases of Egypt which you have known, but will lay them on all those who hate you." (Deuteronomy 7:15 NKJ).

"Bring all the tithes into the storehouse, that there may be food in My house, and try Me now in this," says the Lord of hosts, "if I will not open for you the windows of heaven and pour out for you such blessing that there will not be room enough to receive it". (Malachi 3:10 NKJ).

"Bless the Lord, O my soul; and all that is within me, bless His holy name! Bless the Lord, O my soul, and forget not all His benefits: Who forgives all your iniquities, Who heals all your diseases, Who redeems your life from destruction, Who crowns you with lovingkindness and tender mercies, Who satisfies your mouth with good things, so that your youth is renewed like the eagle's". (Psalm 103:1-5 ESV).

"He sent His word and healed them, and delivered them from their destructions. Oh, that men would give thanks to the Lord for His goodness, and for His wonderful works to the children of men!" (Psalm 107:20 NKJ).

"The Lord is for me among those who help me; therefore I shall see my desire on those who hate me. It is better to trust in the Lord than to put confidence in man". (Psalm 118:7 NKJ).

"I call heaven and earth as witnesses today against you, that I have set before you life and death, blessing and cursing; therefore choose life, that both you and your descendants may live". (Deuteronomy 30:19 NKJ).

"With long life I will satisfy him, and show him My salvation" (Psalm 91:16 NIV).

"But He was wounded for our transgressions, He was bruised for our iniquities; the chastisement for our peace was upon Him, and by His stripes we are healed". (Isaiah 53:5 NKJ).

"'For I will restore health to you and heal you of your wounds,' says the Lord, 'because they called you an outcast saying: 'This is Zion; no one seeks her'". (Jeremiah 30:17 MSG).

"Assuredly, I say to you, whatever you bind on earth will be bound in heaven, and whatever you loose on earth will be loosed in heaven. Again I say to you that if two of you agree on earth concerning anything that they ask, it will be done for them by my Father in heaven. For where two or three are gathered together in my name, I am there in the midst of them" (Matthew 18:18–20 KJV).

"And they were astonished at His teaching, for He taught them as one having authority, and not as the scribes. Now there was a man in their synagogue with an unclean spirit. And he cried out, saying, 'Let us alone! What have we to do with You, Jesus of

Nazareth? Did you come to destroy us? I know who you are—the Holy One of God!'" (Mark 1:22–24 NKJ).

"I, even I, am He who blots out your transgressions for My own sake; and I will not remember your sins. Put Me in remembrance; let us contend together; state your case, that you may be acquitted" (Isaiah 43:25–26 NKJ).

Fasting

Fasting and juice fasting are good ways to detox and to give your body a break from that overload feeling. High toxins and fats cause weight gain, which bogs you down.

Ron Lagerquist, who has written several books on fasting, has studied the subject for thirty years. He lectures widely, sharing his research on a healthy diet and on being God's best with anyone who will listen.

He notes that fats, toxins, and chemicals build up in the body over time through foods you eat and hygiene and cleaning products you use.

Lagerquist says fasting is the only way to detox because:

> The truth of the matter is the North American diet never allows the body to cleanse itself. We eat all the time. The math is simple. When intake of calories is greater than burned, the results will be stored body fat. It is the same with toxins. When intake of toxins is greater than removed, the results will be toxic overload.
>
> If you are overweight this is a pretty good sign you are carrying around a storehouse of toxins, affecting normal cell functions. What happens if the toxic-load is greater than the internal-caretaker can remove? Sickness, weakened immune system and premature death, the plagues of our modern lifestyle.

He says fasting gives your body a break. Lagerquist points to the mini fast your body takes when you sleep at night. When you go to sleep, the work of detoxification begins. The symptoms of detoxification are not pleasant. They include foul-smelling breath, a coated tongue, a fuzzy brain, and puffy skin. The buildup of toxins takes time and so will cleansing yourself. The benefits of detoxification are many, and juicing is a good way to accomplish a healthy detox.

Neutralizing, transforming, and eliminating are three ways we rid our bodies of toxins. God made our bodies with built-in cleansing systems. The liver transforms toxins. The blood carries waste away. Elimination through the bladder, intestines, and sweat glands is important. If these systems are working the way God intended with the right foods and fewer toxins taken in, we will be healthy.

Eliminated during the detoxification process:

- Dead, dying, or diseased cells
- Unwanted fatty tissue
- Trans-fatty acids
- A hardened coating of mucus on the intestinal wall
- Toxic waste matter in the lymphatic system and the bloodstream
- Toxins in the spleen, liver, and kidneys
- Mucus from the lungs and the sinuses
- Embedded toxins in cellular fibers and deeper organ tissues
- Deposits in the microscopic tubes responsible for nourishing brain cells
- Excess cholesterol

The result:

- Mental clarity is improved.
- Rapid, safe weight loss is achieved without flabbiness.

- The nervous system is balanced.
- Energy level is increased.
- Organs are revitalized.
- Cellular biochemistry is harmonized.
- The skin becomes silky, soft, and sensitive.
- There is greater ease of movement.
- Breathing becomes fuller, freer, and deeper.
- The digestive system is given a well-deserved rest.

People testify that after making changes for better eating, fasting becomes easier. Fasting is a measure of lifestyle.

Methods of detoxification

Juice fasting

This is the best choice for detoxification because it supplies an abundance of nutrients, including enzymes and calories to reduce the cleansing intensity to a more comfortable level. Using an enema during a juice fast will flush the lymphatic system attached to the lower colon with water and help remove hardened fecal matter from the intestinal wall while giving the digestive tract an opportunity to rest and to heal.

Water fasting

Water fasting demands more discipline than other forms of fasting.

Raw food diet

A raw food diet of fruits and vegetables will produce the same cleansing reaction as a juice fast, but the process is slower because your system must break down and digest these foods.

Eating less

This is a good way to start the detoxification process, but it can require the greatest discipline. Chewing your food many times and eating smaller amounts help with digestion.

Vegetarian eating

A light vegetarian diet will also help with detoxification. The day's menu might include fruit for breakfast, a salad for lunch, and a meal of cooked vegetables with raw nuts or beans and brown rice for dinner.

Exercise

Walking, stretching, and light exercise can benefit the body during a juice fast or a cleansing diet.

Detoxification aids

To assist the cleansing process, I recommend fresh juice made with a juicer. This a good way to get vitamins and nutrients immediately. You can change the way the juice tastes by using different fruits and vegetables.

Apple cider vinegar

Apples are packed with beneficial vitamins and minerals. Apple cider vinegar is purifying. It reduces inflammation in the body, which is important since inflammation can lead to and feed sickness. This in turn helps support organ function.

Apple cider vinegar can used as a hot or cold beverage sweetened with honey, but it is best used in its natural liquid form.

When the body lacks certain minerals or salts, ill health can result.

Forgiveness and health

Some people ask, "Doesn't forgiving someone mean you're forgetting or condoning what happened?"
The answer is, absolutely not! You can't forget what has been done to you. It will always remain a part of your life, but you can shape how it affects your life. Forgiveness can lessen its grip on you and help you focus on positive parts of your life. You can forgive a person without excusing the act.

What are the benefits of forgiving someone?
Researchers have become interested in studying the effects of forgiving and refusing to forgive those who cause hurt. There is mounting evidence that holding on to grudges and bitterness results in long-term health problems. There are numerous benefits to forgiveness, including:

- Lower blood pressure
- Reduced stress
- Low hostility
- Better anger management skills
- Lower heart rate
- Lower risk of alcohol or substance abuse
- Fewer depression symptoms
- Fewer anxiety symptoms
- Reduced chronic pain
- Increased friendships
- Healthier relationships
- Greater spiritual well-being
- Improved psychological well-being

How do I know it's time to try to embrace forgiveness?
Our lives can be so wrapped up in the wrong that has been done to us that we can't enjoy the present. Other signs that it may be time to consider forgiveness include:

- Dwelling on the events surrounding the offense
- Hearing from others that you have a chip on your shoulder
- Being avoided by family and friends because they don't enjoy being around you
- Having angry outbursts during the smallest interaction with others
- Often feeling misunderstood by others
- Drinking excessively, smoking, or using drugs to try to cope with the pain in your life
- Having symptoms of depression or anxiety
- Being consumed by a desire for revenge
- Automatically thinking the worst about people or things happening around you
- Feeling that your life lacks meaning or purpose
- Feeling at odds with your spiritual beliefs

The bottom line is that you may often feel miserable.

How do I reach a state of forgiveness?
Forgiveness is a commitment to a process of change. It can be difficult and it can take time. Everyone moves toward forgiveness a little differently. It is a choice.

What happens if I can't forgive someone?
Forgiveness can be very challenging. It may be particularly hard to forgive someone who doesn't admit wrong or doesn't express sorrow. Keep in mind that the key benefits of forgiveness are for you.

It can also be beneficial to pray, to use guided meditation, or to journal. In any case, if you have the intention to forgive, forgiveness will come in time.

Caffeine addiction

Caffeine affects your energy and your mood and has long-term repercussions if you develop an addiction to it. In our society, this seems to be an accepted form of addiction. We use caffeine as stimulant to keep us going. My daughter developed an addiction to Mountain Dew in her high school years and relied heavily on this caffeinated soft drink for late-night studies during college. She still struggles with it today in her thirties. Her breast-feeding days with her children were very hard on her.

Withdrawal from caffeine has unpleasant effects on those wishing to end intake or simply to cut back.

High levels of caffeine can produce caffeine toxicity, which has serious consequences.

Sleep disruption, restlessness, large amounts of urine, stomach problems, palpitations, a foggy brain, and bloating are common ones.

Reduce or eliminate caffeine consumption slowly. You must gradually wean yourself off of caffeine to keep the unpleasant effects at a minimum.

Caffeine is not completely bad since it can be used to peak brain activity. Moderate use from morning to midday is fine as long as you don't feel that you need it every day.

Deworming

Deworming is another way to rid the body of a cause of illness. This is not a pleasant subject, but it is worth mentioning.

Deworming is very important. As a child I was dewormed at school after a long barefoot summer. The practice went away, but the worms didn't, and I dare say we have more bugs now than we did then. Parasites can cause problems with the stomach, bowels, digestive tract, heart, head, and skin. They even show up on an X-ray as cancer. If you eat meats and vegetables, go barefoot, have an animal, or put your hands in your ears, nose, mouth, or eyes, you may have parasites that must be eliminated.

The best way to rid your body of parasites is with a combination of black-walnut tincture, ground cloves, and crushed wormwood.

Recipe for black walnut tincture

In the fall, collect black-walnut hulls recently fallen from trees. Select only hulls that have less than 50 percent black discoloration. The greener the better. Do not use cracked hulls. The walnut is inside, but the whole ball must be used since the active ingredient is in the green outer hull. Black-walnut hulls may look and smell like small limes.

Assemble:
- Your largest stainless steel or glass (not aluminum, ceramic, plastic, enamel, or Teflon) pot or bowl
- Black walnuts in the hull, each one at least 50 percent green, enough to fill the pot to the top
- Grain alcohol, about 50 percent strength, or regular vodka, enough to cover the walnuts
- Vitamin C powder (Capsules are fine.)

Caution: black walnut hulls can stain countertops and clothing and may cause contact dermatitis. Handle carefully.

Directions:
Wash the walnut hulls carefully with water for a couple of minutes. Put them in the large- mouth glass container and cover completely with the alcohol or vodka.

Sprinkle on one teaspoon of vitamin C. Cover with the airtight lid or covering and let set for three days.

Add another teaspoon of vitamin C. Use a funnel to pour the tincture into glass bottles, preferably amber bottles. If amber is not available, store the tincture in a dark place. Better yet, store it in a freezer.

Discard the walnuts. (Squirrels love them!)

The vitamin C helps to keep the color green. The tincture's potency will remain strong for several years if the bottles are unopened, even if the tincture darkens slightly.

Walnut tips

When preparing the walnuts, wash only with cold tap water. Rinse with distilled, unfiltered water to remove all chlorine. You may need to use a brush on areas with dirt. The the glass container of soaking walnuts should not be refrigerated.

Tips for reducing exposure to air

Exposure to air causes the tincture to darken and to lose potency very quickly. To reduce air exposure, fill the glass container as much as possible while still allowing the lid to fit snugly. To reduce repeated exposure to the air once a container is opened, it is better to put the tincture in many small bottles rather than one large one. Store the bottles in a dark closet or cabinet or a freezer for maximum potency.

Crushed cloves

They can be bought in a power form at a health food store. You should also be able to buy them anywhere you buy herbs. The fresher the better. You can also purchase empty capsules and put the clove powder in them.

Wormwood

Wormwood can also be purchased at a health food store. I am not sure you can buy this item at the supermarkets where you find other herbs. Fill capsules the same way you do with cloves.

Note: you can find a combination of black-walnut tincture, crushed cloves, and wormwood at a good health food store, but you won't get the same results as you would with fresh ingredients. Do the best you can.

Drinking four to five ounces of spring water with a quarter teaspoon of aluminum-free baking soda is the fastest way to be alkaline neutral, the healthiest state for your body.

You might also try one teaspoon of apple cider vinegar in a half cup of spring water.

You can heat spring water in a microwave and add one teaspoon of apple vinegar and two tablespoons of pure honey. This makes a great tonic for soothing a sore throat or a cough. This mixture also provides energy among other great benefits.

Juicing

Juicing allows all the nutrients, minerals, and vitamins in each juiced item to enter your system sooner. Solid foods must be broken down and digested.

You will have to retrain your taste buds because they have been rewired for sugary foods. This may take a while, but the good health you experience will make the effort worthwhile. Cleanup is a consideration in juicing. Some juicers are better than others, but you must be committed to becoming healthier.

A good juice to start with consists of three carrots and one apple. I always juice with three carrots, a half bell pepper, one cucumber, two stalks of celery, a huge handful of seeded grapes, one apple, two large leaves of kale, and a stalk of broccoli.

This makes two large glasses of juice. I also put a tip of a teaspoon of powdered turmeric in my glass of juice before drinking.

Below I have listed most of the fruits and vegetables that I juice for breakfast. I have also listed the main vitamins and nutrients in each.

Apples- high in vitamin C.

Carrots- Beta-carotene is absorbed in the intestine and converted into vitamin A during digestion. Carrots also contain fiber, vitamins E and K, potassium, folate, manganese, phosphorous, magnesium, and zinc.

Grapes- a rich source of micronutrient minerals like copper, iron, and manganese.

Bell peppers- vitamins A and C, potassium, folic acid, and fiber.

Celery- folic acid (provides 9 percent of RDA), riboflavin, niacin, and vitamin C; an excellent source of vitamin K.

Cucumber- vitamins C and K, B vitamins, copper, potassium, manganese, and beta-carotene.

Kale- vitamins A, C, and K as well as minerals like copper, potassium, iron, manganese, and phosphorus.

Spinach- vitamin A (in the form of carotenoids), manganese, folate, copper, calcium, and vitamins B2, B6, C, E, and K.

Broccoli- vitamins C and K, chromium, and folate. It is a very good source of dietary fiber, pantothenic acid, vitamins B1, B6, and E, manganese, phosphorus, choline, vitamin A (in the form of carotenoids), potassium, copper, magnesium, omega-3 fatty acids, protein, zinc, calcium, iron, niacin, and selenium.

Flaxseed oil

Flaxseed oil has many benefits. I find that my skin is clearer when I use it every day. Some research has shown the use of flaxseed oil reduces the size of tumors.

As I said, this is a lot of information. It took me about eight years to do the research, to absorb this, and to apply what I learned. Take the parts that speak to you and leave the others out.

Whatever you decide, I believe the most important thing you can do to improve your health is to detox—to remove from your system the built-up chemicals to which we are all exposed each day.

Then start juicing fruits and vegetables. You will feel the results of cleaning your system out, and you will have much more energy.

This will not be easy. It will require a lifestyle change, and that is hard for anyone. If you have cancer, it is in a sense chosen for you. Do what you can and God will do the rest. He has proven that to me time and time again.

Blessings to you.

CPSIA information can be obtained
at www.ICGtesting.com
Printed in the USA
FFOW03n1349310117
31955FF